Eve Queler

A View From the Podium

A Memoir

Library of Congress Control Number: 2018913688
ISBN: Hardcover   978-1-9845-6683-6
                Softcover   978-1-9845-6682-9

Cover photo by Christian Steiner

Unless otherwise credited, all photos are courtesy of the author.

Eve Queler caricature courtesy of the Samuel Norkin family.

Print information available on the last page.

Rev. date: 01/24/2019

To order additional copies of this book, contact:
Xlibris
1-888-795-4274
www.Xlibris.com
Orders@Xlibris.com
779049

Contents

Foreword

The first time I saw Eve conduct, I remember being absolutely taken by her rapport with the orchestra. I had not yet met her, but I felt an immediate connection. That was in 1970. Soon thereafter, I became her manager.

Eve was one of the early lights in the progress of women in the male-dominated field of conducting in classical music. She invigorated the rediscovery of opera repertoire, covering works of the Italian, French, and Slavic schools from the early 1800s through the first half of the twentieth century. As a musician, Eve brought something uniquely her own to each performance. As an organizer and casting manager, her knowledge and instincts were uncanny. Unfailing in her selection of singers, she always knew the right vocal quality for the role, for the concert hall, and for the group she was assembling. Her astute ear resulted in the launching of numerous careers.

When Eve formed the Opera Orchestra of New York (OONY), it was as much out of her need to have a platform from which to develop her conducting and improve her techniques, as it was out of a need to create a group of professional musicians from the extraordinary pool of classically trained instrumentalists in the New York area. These young musicians were familiar with symphonic orchestral repertoire, but not with the orchestral literature of opera. Up to that point, orchestra musicians learned the scores of operas when they joined an opera company or for a singular opera production, and rarely arrived trained in the various operatic styles.

Eve's concentration at first was on standard repertory pieces, with rehearsals and performances in a public school in Manhattan. She moved quickly to Alice Tully Hall, making the leap to Carnegie Hall only one year later, opening with Rossini's *William Tell* featuring Nicolai Gedda as Arnold and Louis Quilico as Tell. Gedda became ill for the opening, and Eve showed her impresario mettle by casting not one but two tenors to sing the performance, Mallory Walker taking the more cantabile sections of the role, and the amazing Jerome Lo Monaco confronting the more vocally challenging of Arnold's music, including the grand duet with the soprano and the tenor's aria and cabaletta with innumerable high Cs. Even with Gedda's cancelation, the performance was received as one of the most exciting of the New York opera season.

A second production of Meyerbeer's *L'Africaine* sung in Italian featuring Richard Tucker, Antonietta Stella, and the NY debut of Matteo Manuguerra was also scheduled. The success with public and press was notable, and Eve and OONY were on their way.

Eve saw that by concentrating on the lesser-known works of the great operatic composers, she could offer new vehicles to many opera superstars of the period, while discovering innumerable new talents that emerged from these performances. Eve's contribution to the opera community in her rediscovery of neglected works is incalculable. Her performances included French grand opera, the bel cantistas of the romantic Italian school into Verdi and his contemporaries, such as Boito and Ponchielli, into Puccini, the Italian impressionists and the veristas. She also opened a path for the Russian and Slavic works, which were largely out of the standard repertoire in most Western opera houses. Opera Orchestra's performance of Smetana's *Dalibor* with Nicolai Gedda created great interest in the works of the Czech repertoire. It was a performance of Dvořák's *Rusalka* in Czech by Opera Orchestra which launched a worldwide revival of that opera. OONY's now historic performance of the Janáček masterpiece, *Jenůfa*, again in the original Czech, featured the great singing actress Leonie

Rysanek in the formidable role of Kostelnička, and the great Czech soprano Gabriela Beňačková in the title role. This work had been revived at the Met in an English translation earlier, but never grabbed the public until this Opera Orchestra performance.

Eve has been honored by the Czech Republic, France, and Italy for the interest she created in the artistic legacies of those countries. She was also honored by the National Endowment of the Arts for her lifetime achievement in opera.

Eve is a strong personality capable of incredible focus. The essence of this focus is a strong, convinced sense of purpose and of love—love of the human voice, of music, opera, and family and those she chooses to bring into that family. Family is defined by more than the biological group; rather it includes those Eve inspires and those she elevates with her ideas.

We've been together a long time, Eve and I, and I can say that my years with her and OONY have provided me with some of the most thrilling evenings of opera and singing that I've ever encountered.

Eve, thank you so much for bringing me along.

Bob Lombardo

photo by Liz Queler

March 1999. Arriving for the first full-cast rehearsal of Opera Orchestra of New York's I Masnadieri, *at conductor Eve Queler's apartment on the Upper West Side of Manhattan, I seem to have walked in on an informal luncheon gathering. A field of cold cuts well picked over occupied the massive dining room table. People are scattered in little groups sitting around the table or sprawled in armchairs and sofas in the adjacent living room, following their scores, sipping coffee, talking quietly, even passing around a tiny baby, Queler's two-month-old grandson Joey, who submits with good grace to Paul Plishka's attempt to show him how to walk. Perched on a stool in the crook of the grand piano, Queler leads the music, and rehearsal pianist/assistant conductor Doug Martin, with exact movements of her baton. And standing in the high arch of the double doorway in front of her, Dmitri Hvorostovsky is singing his heart out. This is my kind of party.*

—Anne Midgette, *Opera News*

 **Preface**

It was a cool April morning in 1985. Malcolm, my new secretary, had just arrived at my apartment. I was getting ready for a lunch date with a magazine editor to discuss an article I was writing. Suddenly, Malcolm rushed in to tell me he heard fire engines. I assured him he would get accustomed to those sounds in New York.

"NO!" he said, "the fire engines are right outside!" I hurried to the window; I smelled smoke and saw firemen running into the building. When I opened my front door, I saw only black. I quickly closed the door to gather my thoughts, told myself I was simply hysterical and imagined this, and carefully opened the door again. This time, thick smoke began to enter the apartment. I could see nothing but heard my neighbor next door shouting: "Help, get us out of here, the fire is on nine!" I wanted to go look for him, but I was afraid I would be unable to find my apartment door again.

I ran to the window and shouted nine floors down to the firemen, "We're stranded here! What should we do?" We were told to remain near the window. I ran for the fire extinguishers while Malcolm gathered washcloths and towels. As we closed the doors and stuffed towels under them, my mind raced: would I rather burn up in the fire or jump out the window? Should I call my husband? What if I should die without saying goodbye to my children? It seemed like forever until we heard a voice on the bullhorn saying that the fire was out. Sometime during that forever, I decided I should write a book. Okay, things got busy and some time passed, but thirty short years later, here we go.

1 - Early Years

I was born into a home with a beautiful Mason and Hamlin baby grand piano. My early memories were of my parents making music that I could hear from my room. My mother loved to sing semi-classical songs to my father's accompaniment. One of her favorites began with the words "I have opened wide my lattice." On occasion my parents would hold musicales in our home. I began piano lessons at age five, and soon was able to participate in these evenings with a Chopin Nocturne or Prelude. I still have that piano.

I attended P.S. 64 on Walton Avenue and 171st Street in the Bronx. One day in fifth grade, a classmate of mine, a pretty girl named Roberta Peterman, sang a song called "Waiting" at one of our assemblies. I remember the name of the song because the accompanist was late and we were all *waiting* to hear "Waiting." He finally arrived, wearing tails for the occasion, and flipped them over the back of the piano bench as he sat down to play.

What a beautiful voice! I invited her to my home to sing for my mother. This she did to my accompaniment on the piano. My mother wept at the beauty of her voice and said, "Someday you will sing at the Metropolitan Opera!"

Ten years later, my mother's prophecy came true. Roberta made her debut at the Met in the role of Zerlina in the opera *Don Giovanni* by Mozart. Roberta and I remained classmates through junior high school and traveled together on the subway to Manhattan to audition for the High School of Music and Art. I was accepted but Roberta, with that beautiful voice, was not!

She dropped out of school entirely and began frequent voice lessons with William Pierce Herman. She changed her name to Roberta Peters, and the rest is history.

At age twelve, my beloved teacher, Bea Matter Laurain, arranged for me to audition for the great Madame Isabella Vengerova, who taught at the prestigious Curtis Institute in Philadelphia. My mother and I went to the audition held at her home on 88th Street and West End Avenue. I played Chopin's "Revolutionary Étude" and some other pieces for this gracious lady, after which she said to my mother, "She is very talented. I will take her on as a student and the lessons will be free." Madame Vengerova lived and taught in New York, but she could only give me the scholarship if I took my lessons at Curtis. To my dismay, my mother replied that she would not allow me to travel to Philadelphia alone and could not accompany me because of her obligations at home. I remained silent all the time thinking, "My mother is ruining my life. Why am I not saying anything?"

Madame Vengerova placed me with her New York-based assistant teacher Mildred Jones, a cruel and exacting woman. Miss Jones's first action as my teacher was to insist I remove myself from a piano competition in which I had already reached the final round. During the nine brutal years I studied with her, she never offered a positive word. Luckily, I was resolved in my great love for music; and while I suffered under her tutelage, I credit those years for the backbone and determination I carried through my career.

On the bright side, staying in New York allowed me to enter the fabulous High School of Music and Art (now LaGuardia High School). The school had 1,200 students, half music and half art. Of the 600 music students, 300 sang in choruses and the other 300 played in orchestra. I played French Horn and rehearsed with the orchestra forty-five minutes every day. Our favorites were Brahms and Wagner. Our school song was the main melody from the fourth movement of Brahms' "First Symphony" and our graduation march was the overture to Wagner's *Die Meistersinger*.

During those four happy years, I was introduced to Hugo Wolf's songs, studied German during my lunch hour, and began to attend the Metropolitan Opera as a standee or at a score desk on the top balcony. The Met had a few seats in the fifth balcony with a stand for music, and a light with which a student could follow the score. We could see only a small part of the stage but we could see the conductor. My life was dominated by Wagner, Brahms, and my piano lessons. Every day after school, I would practice the piano for four or five hours and listen to my father's Caruso recordings. I was amazed that the voice could do so many expressive things that the piano could not. By age eighteen, I had abandoned any thoughts of a solo career to pursue my love of the voice and accompanying singers.

Weekends were busy. I loved to roller skate and spent Friday nights and Sunday mornings at the rink, where I figure skated and danced with a partner in the shows. Saturday mornings I played for dance classes, but I always eagerly awaited the Saturday afternoon radio opera broadcasts from the Met. Saturday nights were date nights. One Saturday, my boyfriend at the time came to my home early to keep me company while I listened to the opera. He wanted to talk, but I was

Eve third from left

totally immersed in the broadcast, even the intermission features. Frustrated to tears, he stormed out of the apartment just as Don José was stabbing Carmen, and I heard him say, "Give up music and marry me." I didn't do either.

Soon I began to purchase the scores of the Saturday broadcast operas so I could listen to them with the music in front of me. By that time, I knew that my life would be involved with opera.

On my first day at City College of New York (CCNY), I met Stanley Queler. We chatted for a bit but I didn't give it further thought. However, the next day, Stanley found me in the lunchroom and flashed some concert tickets at me. As news editor of our college newspaper, he often received perks. I accepted his invitation to attend a concert by a leading pianist at Town Hall.

While I was going to college, I had many jobs, including playing for Sunday School, ballet and tap classes, as well as gift wrapping in a haberdashery store. Summers I worked at children's camps where I was a music counselor from the time I was sixteen. I remember putting together *Finian's Rainbow* and several Gilbert and Sullivan operettas with the children: *The Mikado, Pirates of Penzance, and HMS Pinafore*.

The year after we met, Stanley began law school. He was in the first class at the new law school at NYU that had just been built. There was no time for any outside work, only study, which would occupy his next three years. Once we married on December 23, 1951, it was up to me to earn enough for us to live. We visited each parent once a week. Stanley's mother would prepare a wonderful meal for us, always sending home enough of her delicious stuffed cabbage to last a week. My mother would give us uncooked steaks or maybe a whole roasted chicken, so we did not starve. Stanley found us an apartment in the Chelsea area so he could walk to NYU.

I left CCNY after two years and entered The Mannes School of Music. While there, I took a year of vocal accompanying, which confirmed even more that I wanted to spend my life working with singers. I fell more and more in love with the voice and the repertoire of opera and song. My professor Paul Berl was the accompanist for Victoria de los Angeles. He encouraged me to fulfill my dream, but added, "By the way, no one will hire you because women aren't doing this."

By that time, however, I was hooked. I began to accompany voice lessons in the studio of Martial Singher. These were wonderful years for me as I learned the French repertoire from a Frenchman. I also met Louis Quilico, who was one of his students, and would later star in *William Tell,* my first opera at Carnegie Hall with Opera Orchestra of New York (OONY).

It was curious. Sometimes Mr. Singher's students would discuss in my presence that they needed an accompanist, but they would never ask me. I finally asked Mr. Singher if he was satisfied with my work. He said I was wonderful, so I asked him why he had not invited me to accompany him at a concert. He said, "But my dear, you are a woman!" It wasn't just the men. Female singers at the time were also unwilling to perform with a woman accompanist. Some thought two women in gowns looked unprofessional. In fact, the only time a female singer hired me was to accompany her at a concert for the blind!

I had finally left Miss Jones to study with the Mannes piano teacher Olga Stroumillo, Mme. Vengerova's other assistant. Piano lessons, a requirement toward my piano major, were $7 through the school. As I was already studying privately with Mme. Stroumillo at $3 a lesson and paying for everything myself, the extra money was unavailable to me at that time. So despite the fact that I took the lessons and completed all the required coursework, I never received a diploma.

In the summer of 1954, I was a Fellow at Tanglewood, where I was rehearsal accompanist for *The Tender Land* by Aaron Copland, and was thrilled to meet him and work with him. He autographed a page of the score for me, which I treasure.

In 1957, I formed a small company called The Opera Players, to present opera excerpts. Our brochure was entitled "The Opera Players Present Opera Miniatures." Our first venture was *Carmen,* staged, with costumes and the four principal characters. We performed in the Poconos and in various locations in Westchester.

Opera Players (Eve pregnant at piano) with Liz Cole

While a student at Mannes, I volunteered my services to the opera department. Felix Popper, the department head, liked the way I played and introduced me to Julius Rudel at New York City Opera (NYCO). I auditioned for him, and he hired me to play and coach in his first season as music director in the fall of 1957.

2 - Next Steps

photo Sedge LeBlang © Metropolitan Opera

In the summer of 1963, I was music director of the Lake George Opera in New York, which performed with piano accompaniment. My children, Andy and Liz, who were five and three respectively, came along. Andy was given a walk-on part. Liz kept herself busy polishing my nails - while I was playing the piano! Shortly thereafter, I became a rehearsal pianist/assistant conductor at NYCO where I was given the occasional opportunity to conduct piano stage rehearsals. I was delighted to have Andy and Liz join the NYCO children's chorus, as I wouldn't have seen them much otherwise. I was also happy to immerse them in the music that was so important to me.

In the fall of 1967, parents of the children attending the École Francaise in New York City, where Liz was in school, organized a benefit for the school at Carnegie Hall. The chairperson was Vera Stern, wife of the world famous violinist Isaac Stern. Vera and Isaac were parents of three children at École. I performed as did several of the other parents. I played the Ravel *Chansons Madécasses* for Chamber Quartet consisting of piano, flute, cello, and vocalist. I recruited flutist Paul Dunkel and mezzo-soprano Corinne Curry. This was technically my first appearance at Carnegie Hall and my only appearance there as a pianist.

After I played, I joined Stanley in the audience. At one point, Isaac came out onstage to announce the appearance of someone who was not on the program. He said to the audience, "You have to hear this." Out came a seven-year-old cellist, the son of our school's music teacher. As he began to play I was caught breathless! He moved expressively with the music and played with the most gorgeous rich tone. Ten years later, I would conduct him at the Chautauqua Summer Festival in the beautiful Cello Concerto of Edward Elgar. It was such a thrill to work with this lovely person and incredible talent. As my career progressed mostly in the opera world, I did not have another occasion to conduct him, but every time our paths cross I am fortunate to receive a hug. His name was Yo Yo Ma.

In 1965, the Metropolitan Opera National Company was formed, and I was hired as a pianist. An offshoot of the Met, this was a company of young singers who traveled throughout the United States, not to be confused with the Metropolitan Opera which sent productions to several cities each spring. My main assignment was *La Cenerentola.* As I watched with fascination the stylish direction of Gunther Rennert, I began to play improvisations during the action. For instance, when Tisbe ran up the stairs, I would run my fingers up the scale. Dr. Rennert liked that and said, "We keep that. Can you write it down?" On opening night in Clowes Memorial Hall in Indianapolis, I played the accompaniments I had written on the harpsichord. After that I gave my score to the assistant conductor Ed Stahl, who played my recitatives when the company went on tour.

When I returned to New York in September, there was a message from Julius Rudel requesting that I come to the theater that very night to do stage duty for Strauss's *Capriccio,* which I did not know. Stage duty primarily involves standing by the stage manager's desk and following the score in order to cue entrances. Thus began a five-year stay with NYCO during which I assisted on many productions with great singers such as Frances Yeend, Beverly Sills, Norman Treigle, and Phyllis Curtin. One day, I played for a rehearsal with a new artist who would revolutionize operatic life in New York, and the world. The opera was *Carmen* and the tenor was Plácido Domingo. His beautiful, rich, easy voice, superb musicianship, and sunny disposition mesmerized me. He was so natural and friendly that he was immediately embraced by the company. I told my husband Stanley that we had a wonderful new tenor with the amazing name, "Peaceful Sunday." Soon NYCO moved to Lincoln Center and Plácido alternated between NYCO and the Met. When by chance we met between theaters, Plácido always offered a great smile and sometimes even a cookie!

One of my fondest memories is the prologue of Boito's *Mephistopheles* with Norman Treigle singing the title role. The opera began in total darkness. Julius Rudel was on the podium with a lit baton in the dark pit. There were French horns playing from several of the balconies. I played the opening solo on organ from backstage. I had to climb a ladder to reach the organ bench, which sat on a raised platform above the stage. From this position, I could see Julius through a tiny hole in the curtain. Once I reached the organ, the ladder was removed for the duration of the first act, and there I remained!

Below me the children's chorus was singing the tongue twister, "Siam nimbi volanti dai limbi nel santi splendori vaganti." My daughter Liz was in that chorus and remembers those words to this day. This experience gave me many ideas, which I used in my ensuing opera performances, placing brass players and singers in various balconies for effect.

One day I visited Columbia Artists Management and left my name with one of the booking agents for Community Concerts. This was an organization that sent programs by various artists to small communities throughout the United States. The agent looked rather shocked and told me he had never had a request for a woman pianist, but could more readily book me as a conductor. I had been conducting choirs and occasional rehearsals at NYCO and my friend, singer Liz Cole, had been encouraging me down that path as well, so the idea had been brewing for a while. Musically it seemed like the obvious next step, especially since there were so few opportunities for me as a pianist. I made inquiries to Juilliard and Manhattan School of Music. When both institutions said they did not accept women into their conducting programs, I returned to Mannes and began my studies with Carl Bamberger, head of the conducting department. I knew that Julius Rudel had graduated from Mannes as a conductor, so it seemed like a good idea. Looking back, it is remarkable that Maestro Bamberger was willing to open the door when others were not. Opportunities slowly began to present themselves.

3 - Creation of OONY

In 1967, I was an accompanist for the Metropolitan Opera Studio, which sent young singers into schools with one hour versions of *La Cenerentola, Marriage of Figaro*, and other operas that were staged, costumed, and performed with piano accompaniment. At that same time, I formed the Opera Training Orchestra to give musicians experience playing the opera repertoire, and to provide an opportunity for young singers to perform with orchestra. In cooperation with the Metropolitan Opera Studio, we presented a reading of *La Boheme* with orchestra in concert form at P.S. 44 in Manhattan on April 7, 1967. In the audience were people from the National Council of the Met who began taking an interest in our work.

The evening was a success and blossomed into the Opera Orchestra of New York, which in the next two years, would present concert performances of *Carmen, Pagliacci, Madama Butterfly, Barber of Seville, The Marriage of Figaro,* and *Rigoletto.* These concerts were free and began to attract people in the opera world. The singers invited their sponsors, teachers, and colleagues. The performances were also attended by foundations that supported the arts and by people who were interested in young singers.

The morning after *Carmen,* a representative from the Martha Baird Rockefeller Foundation for the Arts telephoned me and told me they would like to support me, and asked if I had a conducting teacher. I had just contacted Joseph Rosenstock, who was conducting at the Met. He told me to prepare the Beethoven First Symphony. "Maybe you can get a job in Podunk with some symphony orchestra. You will never get a job in opera." In the three days between the phone call and my first lesson, I memorized the symphony. After I conducted the first movement for him without a score he said, "I'll teach you opera because you have a chance." The Rockefeller Fund paid for two years of lessons with Mr. Rosenstock.

Word started to get around about my concerts. The opportunity I was offering was very valuable as young orchestra musicians rarely had the chance to learn the opera repertoire. There was plenty of symphonic training available for players, but very little opera. The music schools mostly limited their opera repertoire to material suitable for young singers, which would tend to eliminate Verdi, Puccini, and the French Romantics. We offered these opportunities to the young musicians, using singers who had graduated from conservatories and were beginning to establish their careers. I met many of the singers during my work with the Met Young Artist Program and at NYCO.

Volunteers liked to hang around and help set up chairs and stands and collect the music. Some of these people became box holders when we finally moved to Carnegie Hall. One nice gentleman, Bill Benenson, whom I knew from the Metropolitan Opera Eastern Regional Auditions, said that he thought I should be in a better acoustical environment than P.S. 44 and asked how much Town Hall would cost. The charge was $1000, which Bill agreed to pay. We advertised a free performance of *Don Giovanni*, instructing people to send a stamped, self-addressed envelope to my home address to request tickets. We were swamped with orders. My children and I hand copied the names and addresses which soon became our first mailing list. We did a preview performance at P.S. 44 and then went to Town Hall.

Excitement abounded. The hall was full. The concert was reviewed by none other than Harold Schonberg, music critic of the *New York Times*, who treated us very nicely and called us "youth on the way."

The season following the debut of OONY in Town Hall, Alice Tully Hall opened. I decided to take our orchestra and singers to the new venue. We sent a letter to our mailing list offering two seats to each concert if they would join our "guild" and send a check for $25. Some of our earliest guild members became part of the initial OONY Board.

We were the first orchestra to perform at the Hall. Alice Tully herself attended the performance and afterward came backstage to greet me. A friendship ensued between us, and Alice gave a series of dinners to introduce me to some of the people who would become my sponsors and board members. We performed at Alice Tully Hall for two years with a repertoire that included *Tales of Hoffman*, *Rigoletto*, *Tosca*, *Magic Flute*, *Fedora*, *Belfagor*, and Monteverdi's *Coronation of Poppea*.

4 - The Only Girl in the Class

One day I was accompanying a baritone at the NY auditions for the Seattle Opera. When he finished singing, the director came over to me and said, "I want to offer *you* a job." I assumed it was as a pianist, but I was just beginning to conduct and did not want to accept any jobs that did not include some conducting. In fact, the job offer was to conduct the Silver Series. The Seattle Opera had a Gold Series for which they hired stars, and a Silver Series in which younger artists and covers performed. I was thrilled to receive the offer and thanked Mr. Ross, the director, but explained that I couldn't relocate to Seattle as I had a husband and children in New York. Later that evening, Stanley overheard me recounting the experience to a friend on the phone. "Why didn't you tell me?" he asked. I said there was no reason to discuss it when I could not accept the move. He pointed his index finger at me and said, "We are a couple. If you receive any offers, we talk!" Soon after this, I found myself among twenty hopefuls taking a dictation test at Manhattan School of Music for a conducting program with the St. Louis Symphony. I was the only woman there, and the only one to advance to the final audition in St. Louis.

The audition took place on a Sunday morning. We had received the repertoire three days prior. One of the pieces was the Overture to *The Magic Flute* by Mozart. I had just conducted the entire opera at Alice Tully Hall, so I knew the overture from memory. The other pieces were Rimsky-Korsakov's *Scheherazade* and the second movement of Debussy's *La Mer*. When I arrived at the airport on Saturday night, I discovered my flight was canceled, so I returned home to sleep. At 4:00 a.m., I was awakened by my son, whose sleepover friend had gotten sick. I spent the next couple hours cleaning up the mess and then headed straight for the airport. I got off the plane, barely made it to the audition, and was thrilled to be accepted into the program— the only woman among eight conductors and probably the only one who'd been up all night with a sick child. Interestingly, there was another woman among the finalists. I couldn't help noticing she was dressed in a man's suit and smoked a pipe.

St. Louis Symphony, June 1970
photo by Larry Williams, St. Louis Post Dispatch

It was an intense program, culminating in two concerts. We worked daily with the orchestra and each of us then conducted one quarter of a concert. My assignment was the overture of Berlioz's *Benvenuto Cellini*. What a splendid piece! I learned an enormous amount of symphonic repertoire that month, and had time with the orchestra every day. Toward the end of the workshop, when talent search people came to observe us, I was told, "Of course, no one will be looking at you because none of the orchestras will hire a female conductor." Everyone in that group left with a job except me. One of the men, Mark Starr, was offered two jobs and recommended me for the one he did not accept. So I journeyed to Fort Wayne, Indiana, to be interviewed by the symphony board and was chosen for the position of associate conductor. The music director lived in Indianapolis where he held another conducting post. My duties would be to conduct three of the seven subscription symphony concerts, the one opera, to rehearse the chorus, and to bring the education programs into the schools. Again, I was facing a decision about leaving New York.

I went to Julius Rudel and told him about the post in Fort Wayne. I offered to give up this opportunity and stay in New York, continuing my duties as assistant conductor/coach, if he would give me one performance on the podium. After two weeks, he replied, "The orchestra will never accept you."

Stanley said that if I was serious about conducting, I had to go to Fort Wayne. Before agreeing to leave my family for nine months, I decided to seek out the advice of a prominent woman in the field. I made an appointment to see Helen Thompson, general manager of the New York Philharmonic. "Women can't conduct," she told me. "Perhaps you can conduct Haydn or Mozart, but Brahms and Wagner are man's music." I was so shocked to hear her say this. It seemed surreal. After this meeting, I made two decisions. The first was not to seek out any more advice. The second was to start packing for Fort Wayne. I needed to follow my destiny, and if my destiny was to conduct, I had to go.

5 - OONY Moves to Carnegie Hall

In the late 1960s, I was playing rehearsals for the "Friends of French Opera" at Carnegie Hall, a post that gave me access to some of the biggest names in the opera world. During that time they mounted *Werther* for Nicolai Gedda and *La Juive* for Richard Tucker. Richard was such a gracious man, serious but with a wonderful sense of humor. After the performance of *La Juive,* he hosted a dinner party at the Petrossian Restaurant near Carnegie Hall. Stanley and I were invited, and Richard told his dinner guests that singing *La Juive* had been the dream of his life. He and Nicolai would be the first two superstars to sing with me at Carnegie Hall, and I will always be grateful to them for taking a chance on a fledgling conductor.

When I asked Richard if he would sing an opera with me, he said "Sure, kid" and chose Meyerbeer's *L'Africaine*. Later that year, he invited me to join his family in Florence, where he would sing Verdi's *Un Ballo in Maschera* with the young Riccardo Muti, whom he called "my boy!" There I got to know Richard's wife Sarah and their sons, and was included in some family outings. I recall driving with them to a large villa owned by a fashion designer. When she found out I was a conductor, she decided to make an outfit for me and asked what I usually wore for conducting. I told her I always wore a dress and amazingly, a dress arrived at my home several months later. I don't remember taking any measurements but it fit perfectly!

William Tell - 1972

with Nicolai Gedda   photo by Liz Queler

When I asked Nicolai what he'd like to sing with us, he offered anything on his repertoire list, which included Rossini's *William Tell*. I never knew this was a complete opera, having only heard the overture from the radio show "The Lone Ranger." Intrigued, I chose that opera. Thus began my odyssey searching for the orchestra materials.

The adventure began in Monte Carlo where I went to study conducting with Igor Markevitch. I was the only woman in a class of fifty conductors. At the conclusion of the course, I traveled to Paris to the Bibliotique of the Paris Opera to search for the autograph (the original score, handwritten by the composer) of *Guillaume Tell* as well as *L'Africaine*. Both were written for the Paris Opera. I had only a printed piano vocal score with me. As I looked through a pile at least two feet high of parchment autographs, I discovered at the very bottom a folder marked "Aria for Jemmy," which my score did not include. I exclaimed, "My God, he wrote an aria for Jemmy!"

"Madamoiselle, s'il vous plait, silence ici," whispered the librarian. Jemmy was the name of Tell's son on whose head the apple was placed. There was no indication on the outside of the folder as to where this aria should be inserted, but upon translating the words, "Don't worry, Papa, I'll stand still," I had a pretty good idea.

To my surprise the librarians were willing to copy the aria in the orchestra score for me. I translated it from French to Italian during the return flight to New York.

The rehearsals were going beautifully. I loved working with Nicolai Gedda. He seemed to possess a magical quality and imbued his singing with an otherworldly essence. I could always tell what he wanted to do by his exquisite phrasing and superb musicianship. Several tenors whom I knew asked if they could attend the dress rehearsal on Saturday morning. At that rehearsal, Nicolai did not feel his best and John Gutman, my advisor, said I needed a cover for Nicolai in case his health deteriorated, and he could not sing. I knew that, but I could never find a young tenor who could sing the role of Arnold in *William Tell*. It was an extremely difficult role with many high C's and even a high C#.

I asked each of the tenors at the rehearsal if he would learn one act as a possible cover. One of them agreed to learn the second act. The other knew the first act duet and the big aria in the fourth act. Sunday was then a flurry of coaching. On Monday, the day of the performance and my debut at Carnegie Hall, I received a phone call, "Mr. Gedda is ill and will not be able to sing." I think I went to bed with the vapors!

The manager of one of the covers said that his client would do the performance, but only for the same fee that Mr. Gedda was to receive. I explained that we couldn't do that because he was only singing half of the opera, and I needed to split the fee with the other cover. The manager would not bend. The other tenor was represented by Gedda's manager, from the firm of the legendary Sol Hurok. He said, "Let's just get the performance on! We can discuss the fee tomorrow." I had no choice but to acquiesce to the demands of the first tenor. On the biggest stage, and at the most important performance of my life, I had to personally announce to a sold-out audience the cancelation of Mr. Gedda.

The performance went amazingly well considering that neither of the tenors had rehearsed with the orchestra. The title role was sung by the French-Canadian baritone, Louis Quilico. I knew Louis very well as I had played for his lessons with Martial Singher while at Mannes. He sang the aria that the father sings as he is about to shoot the apple off his son's head with extraordinary passion and pathos. At the end, there was a roar of applause and someone in the audience yelled out, "Quilico, sei un leone!" (Quilico, you are a lion!)

with Antoinetta Stella and Richard Tucker

One month later, on April 20, 1972, I conducted Meyerbeer's *L'Africaine* with Richard Tucker. He had suggested this opera because he knew the aria "O Paradiso." Richard learned the remainder of the role of Vasco da Gama in my studio. I can still picture him standing at the window as I sat accompanying him at the piano. Carnegie Hall was packed. Suddenly, Opera Orchestra and I were on the radar.

I Lombardi - 1972

The evenings spent with Eve and Opera Orchestra of New York are among the happiest memories of the last 25 years. From our first meeting, I felt completely at home. —Renata Scotto

photo by Liz Queler

After our first season in Carnegie Hall, I was contacted by a number of superstars with proposals of operas they wanted to do. The first of these was Renata Scotto who was interested in Verdi's beautiful *I Lombardi alla Prima Crociata*. This performance took place in December of 1972. The bass was young Paul Plishka, who was singing small roles at the Met and would go on to enjoy an illustrious career.

The tenor was someone I had heard several years earlier in Paris, at a concert performance of *Lucrezia Borgia* played by the French Radio Orchestra. His beautiful voice haunted me. I could hardly wait until the lights came up so I could learn his name: José Maria Carreras! He must have been twenty-two at the time. I was thrilled to have the opportunity to hire him for *I Lombardi*.

Two days before the performance, José became ill. Several of us went with him to Dr. Gould, the throat doctor for the stars, who prescribed some medication. We waited on pins and needles until the next day. Dr. Gould gave him the okay to sing, but instructed him to turn on the shower and breathe in the steam. José stayed so long that his watch stopped! Despite the doctor's okay, José's manager urged him not to sing, fearing he would not be at his best in the hall filled with important people. Happily for me, and for the world, José sang, and most beautifully. I loved working with this really sweet person.

We talked about working on other projects together but his career soared so quickly we could never find the time. He left me his personal score of *I Lombardi* which I have given to Michael Fabiano, who sang this role with me recently. I would collaborate again numerous times with Renata Scotto, whom I loved, and with Paul Plishka, who sang with me twenty-eight times in Carnegie Hall!

Soloists top to bottom: Paul Plishka, Will Roy, Franco Marini, José Carreras, and Yoshi Ito. Heinz H. Weissenstein/Whitestone Photo

 **Francesca Da Rimini - 1973**

I was happy and proud to be involved from the very beginning in Eve Queler's achievements, among them Le Cid *and* Francesca da Rimini. *I congratulate her as an excellent conductor and researcher for exciting repertoire.*
—Plácido Domingo

The next opera we did was the exotic *Francesca da Rimini* by the verisimo composer Riccardo Zandonai. I had stayed in touch with Plácido Domingo since first meeting him at NYCO when he sang *Carmen, Pagliacci*, and the Ginastera opera *Don Rodrigo*. I remember pleading with him not to sing *Pagliacci*. I thought he was too young. He said, "Don't worry. I will sing it with my own voice. It will be fine," and of course, he was correct. I also did stage duty for the very atonal *Don Rodrigo*. Plácido's entrance onstage took place with a falcon strapped to his arm. The falconer waited until the last possible moment to strap the bird onto Plácido. It was a big bird and must have been heavy in the leather case, which held the bird's feet. Standing backstage with my pitch pipe, ducking the flapping wings of the frantic falcon, I was tasked with giving Plácido his opening note.

Plácido Domingo and Raina Kabaivanska
Heinz H. Weissenstein/Whitestone Photo

Francesca da Rimini was to feature Plácido, Raina Kabaivanska and the baritone Matteo Manuguerra, whom I had gotten to know during *L'Africaine*. CBS News came to Carnegie Hall to film our dress rehearsal, causing some delays. I realized we would not have enough time to finish rehearsing the last scene, which meant that Plácido would not get to sing the end of the opera at the rehearsal. He asked me how much the overtime would cost and quickly offered to pay for it because he wanted me to be able to finish the rehearsal. I have had a great rapport with a number of singers, but no one had ever before offered to pay for overtime. Plácido is unique.

Francesca da Rimini is full of beautiful music, especially the love theme, which is introduced by a viola pomposa, a cello with six strings. Our principal cellist at the time, Jascha Silberstein, who was also principal cellist at the Met, was able to locate this instrument. It had the most beautiful timbre—wistful yet voluptuous. Zandonai's orchestration also called for the rarely used bass flute. This music made me cry, it was so beautiful. Exiting the stage after Act I, I saw tears in the eyes of Plácido and Raina as well. Several years after the performance, the Met mounted a gorgeous production of this opera featuring Plácido, with Renata Scotto in the title role.

 **The Pearl Fishers - 1974**

I could hardly wait to schedule something else with Nicolai Gedda. This time it was Bizet's *The Pearl Fishers* at Carnegie Hall on January 20, 1974. By this time tickets to OONY performances were sold out, and there were scalpers on the sidewalk. Nicolai sang like an angel. He took the great aria in the first act so slowly and dreamily, I was afraid to breathe lest I break the spell. Nicolai's sound was unique, in part due to how he shaped his vowels, allowing the sound to resonate high in his cheekbones. He used consonants for expression as well, rolling his "r's"—"De mon amourrr prrrofond, j'ai su me rrrendre maitrrre." His upper voice was superb, with a brilliant top, reaching up to a high D. He could also call upon a beautiful pianissimo. He had great command of the many colors of his voice, and his singing was an inspiration.

The soprano was the French singer Christiane Eda-Pierre. She had impeccable style. When baritone Renato Bruson sang the brilliant duet with Nicolai, there was a thunderous ovation. We repeated *The Pearl Fishers* at several other venues around New York. These performances gave some of the covers a chance to sing, and in one of these performances, together with Nicolai Gedda.

Parisina D'Este - 1974

*I remember you always for your kindness, sensibility, and all
the beautiful things you have done.* —Montserrat Caballé

photo by Sandy Speiser
© Sony Music Entertainment

Not long after the success of *L'Africaine* with Richard Tucker, I
received a message saying that Montserrat Caballé would like to meet
with me. What a thrill it was to meet this great singer. She opened
the door of her hotel suite and said, "I have heard about you. I tip my
chapeau to a lady conductor. I want to sing with you." And she knew
exactly what she wanted to sing. It was an obscure opera by Donizetti
entitled *Parisina d'Este*. In those days most of Donizetti's operas
were obscure. Of his seventy-two operas, only four were known: his
most famous, *Lucia di Lammermoor,* as well as *The Daughter of the
Regiment, The Elixir of Love*, and *Don Pasquale*. This request took
me on an interesting search all over Italy for orchestral materials.

Often in the early nineteenth century, operas were written for
specific theaters where composers and singers were in residence.
The orchestra materials then lived at that theater. When the piece was
produced in another town, someone would have to travel to the original

theater to try and find the orchestra parts. On occasion, the composer would rewrite one or more arias or ensembles to accommodate the singers of the new production. In the end, to construct a critical edition (a score reflecting Donizetti's original intentions), I had to write out a great deal of music by hand.

I learned so much about bel canto singing from working with Montserrat Caballé. She knew exactly which embellishments would suit her voice to perfection. She told me that she could go up to her high register, but not stay there for long periods. She liked to bring her voice down and then bring it back up again. We worked happily together, and the following year, she asked me to do another opera of Donizetti, *Gemma di Vergy*. This time, she arrived with the orchestra parts in her suitcase, so I did not have to do the frenzied work of putting together the music for the orchestra. The performance was recorded live by CBS. Montserrat then invited me to conduct at the Liceu Theater in her hometown of Barcelona. The opera was Verdi's *I Vespri Siciliani*. This was my first experience conducting a staged opera in a large theater—the Liceu had 2,300 seats. I had conducted *La Boheme* and *Tosca* at the Lake George Opera and at Oberlin, but those were small town theaters seating 500 with a small pit and stage. I was very excited and worked hard on my Spanish in order to speak to the orchestra in their language.

Guido di Monforte	FRANCO BORDONI
El Sire de Bethune	JUAN PONS
El Conde Vaudemont	JORGE CEBRIAN
Arrigo	PLACIDO DOMINGO
Giovanni da Procida	JUSTINO DIAZ
La Duquesa Elena	MONTSERRAT CABALLE
Ninetta	M.ᵃ ASUNCION URIZ
Danieli	DALMACIO GONZALEZ
Tebaldo	JOSE MANZANEDA
Roberto	RAFAEL CAMPOS
Coro General	Cuerpo de Baile

with the cast, including Plácido Domingo, Montserrat Caballé, and Justino Diaz

On the day of the dress rehearsal, a half dozen people from OONY arrived for my debut. I found out only moments before going into the pit to start the rehearsal that they would need tickets to enter the theater. I rushed to the entrance and asked the theater manager to admit them but he refused. Then I ran to the head of the theater, Mr. Pamias, to apologize and ask permission for them to enter. Mr. Pamias was annoyed with me for the delay, and said that surely I must know the procedure, which was the same in every theater. He accused me of a lack of respect for the theater and shouted at me in Spanish and then in French. Finally, Marta Domingo, Plácido's wife, came to my aid and secured the necessary tickets. What a show even before I conducted one note! It took a few seconds for my hands to stop shaking before I could start the overture. Once we began, all went well. Opening night was fabulous. The singers were extraordinary and the audience cheered at every opportunity.

While Montserrat had several exquisite moments of great singing, the piece de resistance was her "Bolero" in the last act. The staging instructions were for her to distribute white flowers to each member of the female chorus as she sang. I realized as I watched her that she had more flowers than there were female chorus members. She saved the last three flowers and threw them to me on the very last note of the aria. The flowers landed on my music. Of course, the audience noticed this, and there was great applause as Montserrat acknowledged me with repeated gestures. She did the same thing at each subsequent performance. At the second performance, the flowers landed on the head of the first violist!

I was invited to the Liceu again several years later to conduct Montserrat in *Parisina d'Este*, which we also performed at the opera in Nice. She had wanted other theaters to present her in this opera with me on the podium, but none of them would accept a woman conductor. I started to cry when she told me this. She said, "Not cry! You the greatest!" She returned to New York to sing with me one

with Plácido Domingo
I Vespri Siciliani, Barcelona 1974

more time in Verdi's *Aroldo.* This concert was also recorded by CBS and marked the American debut of the young baritone Juan Pons.

 **La Favorita - 1975**

I had met Alfredo Kraus in London when I conducted him in *I Puritani* in concert at Royal Festival Hall. I was struck by the ease with which he sang and the almost nonchalance in which his voice rose to the uppermost register with such a sweet color. He was also very easy to work with. I once asked him where he lived. He laughed and answered, "I live on airplanes."

I was thrilled to present Alfredo with OONY at Carnegie Hall the following season in *La Favorita,* with Shirley Verrett singing the title role. Pablo Elvira and James Morris completed the perfect cast for this opera.

Le Cid - 1976

with Grace Bumbry, Plácido Domingo, and Paul Plishka
photo by Roz Levin © Sony Music Entertainment

6 - OONY Development

For many years, OONY operated with no office or professional staff. Huge bulk mailings were handled from my dining room, assembly line style, with my children pitching in to apply address stickers to flyers, which were then sorted and bundled into piles by zip code. Gradually we grew. By 1972, our first season at Carnegie Hall, we had a six-person board in place. Our first few seasons at Carnegie were presented by the Hall, so many of the administrative duties were handled by their staff. Soon enough, however, it became necessary for us to put our own administrative staff together. Thanks to a New York City Comprehensive Employment Training Act (CETA) grant in 1978, we were able to hire four employees—three to help with tickets, and a pianist, Marcia Blackstone, who is my friend to this day. Our first manager was John Broome, a tenor in our chorus, who presented himself to me announcing that he wanted to retire from the lyric stage, admired what I was doing, and wanted to help. John was a very colorful Texan with a great sense of humor, and we had lots of enjoyable times as he learned about organization of rehearsals, ordering music, and coordinating soloists, orchestra, and chorus.

Our *William Tell* experience taught me the hard way that it is imperative to have understudies in place. To that end, we implemented our Young Artists Program, wherein we hired rising talent for our cover cast. The program offered performance opportunities with orchestra, free coaching with me, and a chance to listen to and learn from the greatest singers in the world. It also provided a vehicle for me to keep an eye (and ear) on the pool of emerging singers in the opera world, leading to my reputation for discovering great talent.

7 - Symphony Orchestra Engagements

In the early 1970s, I received a number of invitations from symphony orchestras. These enabled me to enlarge the repertoire I had learned in St. Louis and Fort Wayne. I conducted the Puerto Rico Symphony, Hartford Symphony, New Jersey Symphony, Colorado Springs Symphony, and Jacksonville Symphony in wonderful repertoire including the Shostakovich Fifth Symphony, Stravinsky's Firebird Suite and most of the Beethoven symphonies. I also guest conducted the Montreal Symphony in an Opera Gala, The Paris Radio Orchestra in the opera *Fedora*, the Mostly Mozart Festival Orchestra, and the Toledo Symphony Orchestra in a mixture of opera and symphony.

In 1975, I conducted the San Antonio Symphony. The concertmaster John Corigliano was retired from the same position with the New York Philharmonic. He was extremely supportive of me in my first experience with a major symphony, helping with bowings in the overture to Wagner's *Tannhauser* and Berlioz's *Symphonie Fantastique*. This concert was broadcast nationally and occasioned my invitation to two of our great major symphonies.

 **The Philadelphia Orchestra - 1976**

I was to make my debut with the Philadelphia Orchestra during their summer season at Saratoga. I was planning to open the concert with a beautiful symphonic poem taken from the Richard Strauss opera, *Die Frau Ohne Schatten*. I had conducted this piece recently at Carnegie Hall, loved it, and thought it would be a good introduction for me to that great orchestra.

I was stunned to receive a call one evening from their music director Eugene Ormandy regarding the program. That this esteemed conductor took the time to call me directly was incredibly meaningful to me. Evidently the orchestra materials were less than satisfactory for him, so he requested that I change to the tone poem "Death and Transfiguration" also by Strauss. He was so charming on the phone, telling me how delighted he was that I would be the first woman to conduct a full program with the orchestra.

That summer, as I walked onstage to begin my rehearsal, a member of the first violin section, one of the few women in the orchestra, called out, "Right on!" My rehearsal went beautifully. The principal violist Joseph DiPasquale asked me if I played viola. I told him that I didn't. He said, "You conduct like you do."

Stanley and I decided to stay in a neighboring town, Glens Falls, which I knew from spending several summers conducting the Lake George Opera. Two women picked us up at seven the evening of the performance, which was to begin at eight. Unfortunately, they did not know their way to the concert venue. As this became clear to us, I felt Stanley's clammy hand on mine, trying to reassure me. I did the only thing I could do. I tuned everything out and rehearsed the Strauss in my head. Since I was conducting the program from memory, it couldn't hurt to secure it. I knew the piece lasted approximately twenty-four minutes and hoped when I had finished, we would be at the festival. We arrived at the stage door with only five minutes to spare. The concertmaster, who was waiting for me in my dressing room said, "Boy, you are a cool cookie." Little did he know!

After the intermission, Queler returned to the podium and delivered a Beethoven's Seventh (again scoreless) that any conductor could be proud of. The second movement was nicely paced and unhurried. The conductor was applauded greatly at the conclusion of the performance. She should savor the entire evening because when she returns to conduct again at Saratoga—which she surely should—it will be no big deal. She'll just be one of the boys.
—Bill Rice, The Schenectady Gazette

The Cleveland Orchestra - 1977

I was honored to conduct the Cleveland Orchestra at the Blossom Summer Concert Series. My program in Cleveland featured the famous baritone Robert Merrill. Mr. Merrill wanted to sing a number of arias with an orchestral piece between each number to give him a rest. His choices for arias were "Largo al Factotum" from Rossini's *Barber of Seville*, "Toreador Song" from *Carmen*, "Zaza Piccola Zingara" from Mascagni's opera *Zaza*, and the aria "Non Piu Andrai" from Mozart's *The Marriage of Figaro*.

I chose as my orchestral solos the great overture to Wagner's *Flying Dutchman*, the very difficult overture to *The Bartered Bride* by Smetana, which was a supreme test to the entire string section, and the wistful prelude to Moussorgsky's *Khovanshchina*, which would later be the first Russian opera I would program with OONY. There was also the excellent Cleveland Orchestra chorus under the director Robert Page. We would end the program with the Coronation Scene from *Boris Godunov*. The chorus also sang a very beautiful little-known chorus from Verdi's opera *I Lombardi alla prima crociata*.

A symphony orchestra usually has three or four rehearsals prior to presenting a new program. That program is then repeated several times. In the summer series, there is only one rehearsal per concert. The orchestra plays several different programs each week. Since my program contained some music I thought might be new to them, I requested a meeting with the librarian, to be sure that we were literally on the same page. This meeting took place on Friday night before the Saturday concert.

My one rehearsal was to be the morning of the concert. As I was looking through the orchestra materials to see which bowings were marked, I came to the choral piece "Oh Signore" from *I Lombardi*. Immediately, I saw in the first measure that the wrong instruments were playing the introduction. When I told the librarian, he asked if I had the score. I showed him my score and he said to the other two librarians in the room, "Okay, guys, put up the coffee and get out the pencils." I could not believe what I was hearing. Those three gentlemen stayed up all night to hand copy the proper orchestration.

By way of explanation, this music was not in the library of the Cleveland Orchestra, as they had never played it before, so the music was rented. Obviously, the company which rented out the parts for this choral piece did not have a full orchestra score. They invented an orchestration from a score reduced for piano alone. Their all-night extraordinary effort resulted in an almost perfect reading with exactly one mistake in one of the horn parts, which I was able to correct quickly. I had never seen such professionalism. They could easily have insisted that I use what they had, but they did not.

My experience at the rehearsal the next morning would prove to be most enjoyable. I remember many smiling faces in front of me. Our beautiful selections from the great opera literature and the extraordinarily charismatic performance of Robert Merrill brought much pleasure to the audience.

The Cleveland Orchestra concert at Blossom Music Center last night was exhilarating and very different. Everyone on stage seemed caught up in the joy of making so much appealing music. That gang responded to Ms. Queler's urgings from the podium with great warmth and precision. It was a kind of love-in with the audience being the major beneficiary. Rarely have I heard such a well-balanced and skillfully programmed concert. Ms. Queler, who is founder and conductor of the Opera Orchestra of New York, knows exactly where to find the choice goodies in the giant operatic cookie jar. She knows what music thrills, stirs and melts an audience. Ms. Queler had the orchestra in top form throughout the evening. To say that she was in total command doesn't seem appropriate in her case. One who is in command coaxes and whips. Ms. Queler, I suspect, charms instead. Anyway, she had everyone working as a tightly knit ensemble and the result was glorious music. — The Cleveland Press

The next day, Stanley and I were invited to lunch in one of the oldest clubs in Cleveland. When we arrived at the building, I was instructed to enter through a side door as only men were permitted to use the front door. The night before, I had successfully conducted one of the greatest orchestras in the world, but today—the side door.

8 - Conducting Debut with New York City Opera - 1978

While all the pianist/accompanists at New York City Opera (NYCO) were considered "assistant conductors," only the men actually got to conduct. Nevertheless, nothing could have better prepared me for my life conducting opera-in-concert at Carnegie Hall and Lincoln Center than my years accompanying stage rehearsals with NYCO.

In the late 1960s, the heyday of NYCO, I had the opportunity to play for staging rehearsals for two of the greatest stage directors in the opera world at that time, Frank Corsaro and Tito Capobianco. As rehearsal pianist, I was privileged to hear the conversations between both of these directors and Beverly Sills, Norman Treigle, Plácido Domingo, and many others. The discussions were about the music, the words, the feelings, the characters they were portraying, and what a particular phrase of music could express. These men understood the words they were staging, the plays from which the opera libretto was formed, and the emotional meaning of the text. In those wonderful, amazing years of rehearsals, I learned the texts of the operas, which has served me to this day. I was at the ready to jump in after a discussion, to throw a word to a singer, or play a note. Tito and Frank, very different in personality and approach, always searched for the meaning and the beauty. Working with them highlighted for me the importance of focusing on the words, a practice I have adopted in all my work, be it concert opera, semi-staged, which I did with the gifted Ira Siff, or staged.

Eight years after Julius Rudel told me the musicians would not accept me at NYCO, he invited me to conduct Mozart's *Marriage of Figaro* starring Samuel Ramey in the title role. Sam had sung my *Rigoletto* at Alice Tully Hall ten years earlier, so I was looking forward to seeing a familiar face.

I was happy to have this opportunity, which proved quite challenging. I was given no rehearsal with the orchestra, so I sat in the pit for four performances to study exactly what Julius did. He conducted and played his own recitative accompaniment at the harpsichord. I had conducted *Figaro* before and had also played recitative accompaniments on the harpsichord, but I had never done both together. Putting down the baton to play the harpsichord and grabbing the baton to start the orchestra while standing up without missing a beat, was a challenge.

Unbeknownst to me, this was to be the last season for Julius, so in hindsight, this *Figaro* was a lovely parting gift from him. Before my performance, I received a note from Beverly Sills wishing me well and saying that my debut was "long overdue." At the end of that season, it was announced that Julius would step down and his position would be taken over by Beverly, who would retire from singing. When Beverly took over, I wrote her a note congratulating her and saying that I wanted to be there with her. She answered my note very sweetly saying that I would always be there with her, but she never invited me to conduct.

9 - I Capuleti ed I Montecchi - 1979

I met Tatiana Troyanos while I was coaching at NYCO in 1961. I prepared her for her European audition, and when she returned with a contract from Hamburg, I prepared her in the three roles she was offered: Carmen, Dorabella, and Octavian. I have wonderful memories of working with her in my apartment. My living room is an open space combining the foyer and the dining room. Nice for sound, but tricky when there are toddlers riding their tricycles around. Tatiana was very sweet about the interruptions.

Working with Tatiana was a joy. When she set sail in 1965 for Bremen on the Bremerhaven, my then five-year-old daughter Liz and I went to see her off and attended her farewell party. When we visited her stateroom, a very small room with three bunk beds, I told Liz that Tatiana would sail away in a modest room and return a princess, which she certainly did. It wasn't until 1979 that we reconnected when we decided to do Bellini's *I Capuleti ed I Montecchi*. She appeared at the performance dressed as Romeo, with boots and a cape. I can still hear her divine voice in my head, with its color and uniqueness.

The Giulietta was the stunning Ashley Putnam. Our first meeting was awkward. My appointment with Ashley for coaching the role was the same day that Mariella Devia was scheduled to come to my studio. My manager, Bob Lombardo, had asked me to hear Mariella, as she was in New York to audition for the Met. I had never met her and had no idea what she planned to sing. As luck would have it, Mariella arrived a bit late and Ashley a bit early, causing Ashley to sit in the dining room and listen to Mariella sing. And what had she chosen? "O Quante Volte"—the very same aria that Ashley came to work on!

Despite that unfortunate beginning, once Ashley and I started working, her beautiful voice and the exquisite music took over. She knew what she wanted to do with the role of Giulietta. Ashley, who is tall and striking, appeared at the concert in a gorgeous white gown and sang beautifully.

10 - More Conducting Around the World

 **Prague - 1982**

On the evening of my last performance in Prague, I arrived at the Smetana Theater about forty-five minutes before curtain time to check some last minute details. My first task was to go to the orchestra pit and see that no one had changed the height of my music stand. As I mounted the podium, something gold caught my eye. Tucked under the glaring lights that would illuminate my music in the darkened theater were three lovely roses tied with a gold ribbon. Beneath them was a picture postcard of Prague bearing the words in English, "From the orchestra of the Smetana Theater, Prague." As tears clouded my contact lenses, I began to look back over my stay. Guest conductors were rare in that city and Americans rarer still.

The Czech people are proud of their beautiful capital and of their musical heritage, as well they should be. They welcomed me warmly and graciously helped me as I wandered through the theater's maze of hallways, struggling with the two dozen or so Czech words I knew. Whenever I conducted abroad, I tried to learn enough key words to rehearse the orchestra without a translator. That meant learning the numbers, at least from one to ten, the days of the week, and such simple phrases as "Two measures before number 14 . . ." In addition, of course, I learned how to say good morning, please, thank you, yes, and no. Add this vocabulary to a lot of smiling and singing, and somehow through the universal language of music, I usually managed to convey what I wanted.

The beautiful old Smetana Theater was being used by the National Opera of Prague while their National Theatre was being refurbished. Magnificently decorated, the Smetana seated about

Carmen rehearsal

Smetana Theater
photos by Liz Queler

1,000. Another beautiful theater still in constant use in Prague was the Tyl Theatre, for which Mozart had composed *Don Giovanni*! Luckily, I was able to hear a performance of it there, especially meaningful to me because it was the first opera I ever conducted. Performed and produced on a very high level, it was sung in Italian—the only opera of the seven we saw in Prague not translated into Czech.

My working visit to Prague was one of the most profound experiences of my life. Prague was still under communist rule, and the ideology permeated the citizens' lives and dominated all aspects of society. Red stars and hammer and sickles, hanging over doorways, the stage curtain at the opera, and up and down the streets, were a constant reminder. Armed soldiers were a typical sight, as were lines out the door at the local grocery store (with near empty shelves inside). And yet the people were gracious and lovely.

Accompanying me on this trip were my good friend Leigh Raben and my daughter Liz. The members of the company opened their hearts to me. Some orchestra members had my recordings and asked to have them autographed or for permission to take my picture. The administrative staff presented me with a beautiful picture book about the National Theatre, and sometimes admirers were waiting at the stage door to give me little dolls dressed in traditional costumes.

I had been engaged to conduct performances of *Carmen* and *Rigoletto*. When I was met at the airport by a representative of Pragokoncert, the state arts agency, I was presented with a schedule of my rehearsals, press and radio interviews, and with an envelope containing one-third of my fee in Czech crowns. This was unusual in my experience, but fortuitous as I would need to spend them during my stay. Of course at the time there was no Euro, and Czech crowns were not on the currency exchange market, and thus worthless outside the country. By the time we went home, our luggage was loaded with Czech cut glass.

photo by Liz Queler

The following day I was escorted to the enormous Smetana Theatre with its adjacent rehearsal building. There I met with the chorus master, the concertmaster, and the Czech maestro who had last conducted *Carmen*, my first assignment. They explained the cuts customarily used in the current production, designed by the great Josef Svoboda. The following day, I had my first rehearsal with the soloists. I borrowed the company scores to copy rehearsal numbers, cuts, and a few Czech cue words. At this rehearsal, I learned for the first time that my Carmen was to be an East German guest artist, Uta Burkhardt, who would sing in German while everyone else sang in Czech. This made for some confusion, particularly in the recitatives, but it kept me on my toes. That evening I attended a performance of *Faust* (called *Faust and Marketka*) sung in Czech. The Marguerite (Marketka) was Nadia Sormova, who had sung in my New York performance of Smetana's *Dalibor* a few years earlier.

The production was wonderful. Overall, I was fascinated by the theater techniques and casting strategies at Pragokoncerts. Interestingly, the role of Faust was shared by two tenors, a spinto for the older Faust at the beginning, then a lyric tenor after the transformation. The National Opera was a repertory company. During my stay, I heard Prokofiev's *Flaming Angel*, Dvořák's *Jacobins* and *Rusalka*, and Smetana's *Tajemstvi*, among others. I was also able to attend rehearsals for my beloved *Dalibor*. I observed during the performances that a soloist might do a major part one night and small role two nights later. More than half the soloists were over forty, and a significant number over fifty. It was gratifying to see that singers were not discarded when they reached middle age. Thanks to intelligent casting, these artists remained active and continued to be valuable assets to the company. Eventually at a point agreed upon by the artist, the theater, and the union, they retired with a pension. Sparafucile in *Rigoletto* was seventy-two years old and still going strong with a wonderful low F that went on for days!

During the first few performances I attended, I noticed that it was customary to applaud the conductor only the first time he entered the pit. When he appeared for the second and third acts, he began in silence. Since we witnessed some fine conducting, we decided to put a stop to this practice. We were in a box and started applauding at the beginning of Act 2 as the conductor entered the pit, and we succeeded in getting the rest of the public to join us. We also noticed that the conductor did not appear after the performance to take a curtain call with the singers. I was sort of happy about this because it meant I could conduct in comfortable shoes without having to worry that anybody would see them. At the end of my performance, I went back to my dressing room and put my tired feet up on the couch. A moment later the stage manager came running into my room. "You must come to the stage! You have a big success!" I never had time to change my shoes.

(L) Ambassador Matlock
(R) at the residence
photos by Liz Queler

One of the high points of my visit was a luncheon given in my honor by then US Ambassador Jack Matlock. The residence of the American ambassador to Czechoslovakia was a magnificent mansion. It was built in the 1920s by the Petschek family. It was elegant, with its beautiful wood-paneled walls, a charming music room, an impressive library, and a grand staircase. The other guests were members of the theatre and of the ambassador's staff. Service at lunch was orchestrated so that each person who was serving would line up equally spaced throughout the dining room. When everyone was in place, they began to serve at the same moment. The meal was impeccable. Ambassador Matlock rose to make a speech and amazed me by speaking in Czech. I asked him how long he had been in Prague, and he answered, "Six months." Zdeněk Košler, the director of the Prague Opera and an excellent conductor, then made a very moving speech in English. He said that they were so pleased to have been able to invite me to conduct the National Opera, and that although our countries had not had a great deal of cultural exchange, he hoped this would be the beginning of many years of collaboration. I was proud to have been invited, proud of my country, proud of my ambassador, and happy that in some small way I was doing something positive for my country's relations with this great people.

Now back to those three roses on the music stand. There was a small problem. The roses were beginning to wilt under the hot lights. What to do? Obviously, the orchestra had hoped I would find them when I mounted the podium for the performance. Nobody had expected that I would come early to look around. My love for all growing things didn't permit me to leave them there to wilt during the forty-five minutes before the performance. However, my feelings for the orchestra at that moment prevented me from removing the flowers and thereby spoiling their enjoyment of my surprise. I decided that the flowers would have to hold out and willed them not to dare wilt until I returned. Forty- five minutes later, the flowers were no worse for the wear. I lifted them up and motioned my thanks to the orchestra, turned to thank the audience for their applause, and then turned back to look for a place where I could put them out of the light. I made a little umbrella out of the postcard and began *Rigoletto.*

The trumpets intoned their somber beginning with the "Curse of Monterone," and I looked up at the stage. The curtains had opened, and I saw a silhouette of Rigoletto, his hunchback showing under his cape. As we played the prelude and the trombones joined the trumpets, the silhouette became the actual Rigoletto as he came forward toward me. I was numbed by the power of this opening conception. As the opera began and the stage band began to play backstage, I tried again to adjust the flowers to make them more comfortable, moving them off the music stand and on to the little lighting panel next to the podium. There they remained happy until the first intermission when I could take them to my dressing room. Those roses remained alive for the rest of my stay in Prague.

 **Budapest - 1982**

I love Budapest. It is one of my favorite cities. There was a great deal of warmth and charm. Lovers caressed one another walking along the Danube.

This was my third trip, and it was for the purpose of recording Strauss's *Guntram*. I felt so appreciated there from the yellow roses (sarga virag) presented to me at the airport, to the red roses (piros virag) in my room. From my window at the Hotel Forum, I could see a long stretch of the Danube, three bridges, the Citadel on the other side of the river, and many excursion boats with lettering in multiple languages. I enjoyed wondering where they were going.

The Hungarian State Orchestra musicians were very receptive. My *jo reggel* (good morning) always brought an enthusiastic response. They were probably anticipating my saying something funny in Hungarian, and I'm sure I did not disappoint them. In the rehearsal room at the Vigado Theatre, the orchestra fans out in risers, going quite high in the rear where the tympani were placed, but we could all see each other. We worked together as if we had been doing it for years. Some people spoke a little English and some spoke German. I tried as much Hungarian as possible and between the mélange of languages and my doing a bit of singing, I managed to communicate with both the orchestra and the producers. *Guntram* is a very symphonic opera as are all of the operas by Richard Strauss, and this orchestra being a symphonic orchestra understood the idiom well. As is typical in many of Strauss's works, however, there were some passages which bordered on being unplayable.

I was assigned a driver named Martin. The Hotel Forum was only one block from the Vigado Theatre, but I let Martin drive me so as not to deprive him of two days' work. Thankfully he spoke German as did I, so we could communicate. On my previous visit, my driver Kozma spoke only Hungarian, which was a great challenge.

In Hungary at this time, the basic cost of living was affordable, but luxury items were out of reach for most. An expensive meal could cost a week's salary for some. Concerts and opera were very well attended. Hungary at this time was still under communist rule, and most of the instruments played by the orchestra were actually owned by the state.

The day after we finished the recording, I lost my voice entirely and had a very sore throat. My driver had taken the day off, as I should not have needed him until it was time for me to go to the airport. I secured the name of a doctor and called a taxi from the hotel to take me to the hospital. I still cannot get over how attentive the taxi driver was. He escorted me into the hospital and up to the doctor's office where he waited outside the door. When my appointment was finished, and I showed him that I had a prescription, he drove me to a drugstore, went inside himself, had the prescription made up, paid for it, and just waved me aside when I wanted to repay him. I tipped him well.

A common practice in Hungary was to share a restaurant table with strangers. This was mainly in the inexpensive restaurants where the workers ate. The German tenor Reiner Goldberg and I went together to some of these restaurants.

The Hungarians had a very strong cheese called pálpusztai. Our producer David Mottley of CBS, was very fond of this cheese. It didn't appeal to me at all. I thought it smelled like old socks, but David loved it, and brought some back to England in his suitcase!

Caracas - 1982

I made the trip to Caracas accompanied by my friend and colleague Yveta Synek Graff. Yveta loved to explore. She attended rehearsals but also took off almost every day for some neighboring city or interesting site. I was so glad to have her with me, especially to help fend off the Latin men. I couldn't get used to the fact that a woman alone could not simply stand in a hotel lobby, lest she immediately be approached by a man asking her to dinner.

We stayed at the Anauco Hilton in a duplex with a view overlooking the highway, so we could always tell if we might encounter traffic going to the opera. In order to get to the Metropolitan Theater where my performances of *Lakmé* were taking place, we had to take a taxi. One of the oddest experiences we had with taxi drivers was with one who got disgusted when it started to rain, slowing down traffic. He was so frustrated he actually kicked us out of his cab.

There were three orchestras in Caracas: Orchestra Sinfonica, Orchestra Philharmonica, and Orchestra Metropolitana. We heard the Orchestra Metropolitana in a gala concert the night after we arrived, and were relieved to find that they were not the orchestra I would be conducting. Our orchestra for *Lakmé* was the Orchestra Sinfonica, which we were told was the best. After rehearsals began, I hoped this was not true. Certainly there must be a better orchestra in Caracas. That turned out to be the Philharmonica, quite a well-organized orchestra which included a number of American players whom I knew. The Sinfonica, a full-time orchestra, had some good players, and we managed. The players included people from Poland, Russia, Czechoslovakia, and Romania who had settled in South America. They were the older players. There were one or two younger players who were American, and the rest were from South America.

Yveta and I came to love Venezuelan cuisine and enjoyed a steady stream of fantastic seafood. Although we tried, we couldn't get to all the great restaurants that tempted us. Mariella Devia was the soprano, who had sung *Lakmé* with me at Carnegie Hall. It became Yveta's job to take Mariella out for pasta. Mariella liked to have her pasta at 1pm each afternoon.

The tenor Nicolai Gedda unfortunately canceled just three weeks before the performance. The substitute tenor was an old friend and colleague, Luis Lima. Luis had to learn the part, a difficult one for him because it was a little too light for his voice. The tessitura was placed where it was difficult for him to connect the line, but to his great credit and because of his fine artistry, he managed to give a really good performance.

One of the fascinating aspects of working with international casts was seeing the matters of the world from other perspectives. Our trip coincided with the Falklands Crisis. When Yveta and I arrived, the feeling in Venezuela toward Americans was not very good because, of course, we had sided with the English. Venezuela, although a great ally of the United States, supported the Argentinians. Luis, who was from Argentina, was very troubled by the whole situation, and worried about his country and the conditions there. We had many interesting talks about politics.

The American Embassy in Venezuela was a very active one and invited us to a number of events. Due to our schedule, the only one we could attend was a trip for the wives and families of the Americans stationed in Caracas, to a festival about an hour and a half outside of the city. Yveta and I were both very excited to go. With no prior instructions, we arrived at the embassy at the appointed time. Our journey took us to a very small town in a remote area to see "the dancing devils," who turned out to be performers in papier-mâché masks, dancing and shaking maracas. The town had absolutely no facilities for the thousands of people who had descended on it for this well-publicized festival. There was nowhere to sit, there were no restaurants, just a village green. When we arrived at 11am, our group dispersed with instructions to meet back at the car at 2pm, so we had three hours to wander without much to do. We bought a few masks and looked for a place to have lunch, but with little luck. There was a questionable-looking greasy spoon, but we were advised not to eat there. Ultimately, we went to sit in a pretty little church, the only place to escape the intense noontime heat. We sat there for at least an hour until Yveta suggested we go back to check that the car was still there. Alas! The car was NOT there! This of course made us very nervous, so we decided to search for a phone to call Caracas and ask for a car to pick us up. But first we needed a restroom! Our panic took us to the police station where we found something that was being repaired that resembled a toilet. Finally, we could turn our thoughts back to finding a telephone.

Suddenly, someone from our party came running up to us and said, "We have been looking for you! We have been looking for you!"

We asked, "Where have you been? The car moved."

"Yes," he replied, "we are on the other side of town. We decided to leave early. People wanted to leave and we couldn't find you." So we went racing back.

The company in the car was rather interesting because it included wives and small children of Americans connected to the American Embassy. One family with small children had been through a revolution in Nicaragua, which necessitated them being airlifted from the country. The stories were fascinating and a nice departure from the opera stories to which I was accustomed. We asked the group how they managed in Venezuela with, for instance, not being able to eat salad. Most of them grew their own lettuce, washed it in a combination of Clorox and water, then rinsed it and ate it. One woman told us about her little boy. They had been stationed in Sweden, and he wanted only bananas. He begged and pleaded for bananas. Of course, they couldn't get bananas where they were, so with the greatest of good fortune they were transferred to Caracas, which was abundant in bananas, and, of course, he immediately lost interest in bananas.

Lakmé rehearsals were challenging. There is a certain aspect of the Venezuelan dialect that alters the pronunciation of the letter *s*, and I coached the local singers as they struggled with their French. In addition, their musical preparation was a bit careless. It was difficult to persuade them that quarter notes and dots were important! Luis Lima and Nicola Ghiusalev arrived a few days late due to the fact that the performances they were doing in Buenos Aires had been delayed. Ghiuselev had not had sufficient time to prepare the part and came down with a cold besides, so for two days he was not able to do much. It finally all came together with Mariella, of course, stealing the show. Her "Bell Song" with two fantastic high E's brought the house down at every performance. Singers are often superstitious. For Mariella who had grown quite close to Yveta, she would never sing her high E unless Yveta was in the wings.

with Mariella and Yveta

11 - Back to Carnegie Hall

Tribute to Marion Anderson - 1982

Wedged in between all the traveling in 1982 was the concert I conducted in Carnegie Hall, sponsored by *Ebony Magazine* to celebrate the eightieth birthday of the legendary soprano Marion Anderson. The stage was to be shared by two sopranos, Grace Bumbry and Shirley Verrett. Shirley had sung with me in Donizetti's *La Favorita* several years before. Grace had sung with me in *Le Cid* with Plácido Domingo, recorded live from Carnegie Hall by CBS. There was tremendous anticipation at the prospect of hearing these two great divas on the stage together.

A meeting was held in the library of the Met to choose the arias, and the order in which they would be sung. It was tricky to say the least, to try to satisfy both women, as singing an aria immediately after a duet can be tiring. Although there was no way to make it perfect for both ladies, we found creative ways to have fun with the programming, which included the famous duet from *Norma* in which Grace sang Norma and Shirley sang Adalgisa. They then repeated the duet, switching roles!

with Shirley Verrett, Isaac Stern, Marion Anderson, Grace Bumbry
Photograph by Henry Grossman:/© Grossman Enterprises, LLC

Nabucco - 1984

There is an opera festival in Las Palmas, in the Canary Islands, named after the great tenor Alfredo Kraus, who was born there. In 1978, they invited me to conduct *Elisir d'Amore* by Donizetti. I had the opportunity to hear Ghena Dimitrova, so I remained three days after my last performance to attend her rehearsals. In those three days, she marked at all of the rehearsals, so I never actually heard her sing full out, but I was fascinated by her intensity and the color of her voice. I could tell that it was a huge instrument, so I decided to invite her to debut in New York in the opera *Nabucco*.

with Dimitrova and Plishka

I will allow the critics to describe the effect of her voice on all of us:

"Hers is a voice of tremendous thrust, capable of soaring over the most uproarious of Verdi ensembles. Pressed for comparison, I would say that in amplitude it is somewhere between a Tebaldi and a Nilsson." –Donal Henahan, *The New York Times*, May 15, 1984

"The walls of Carnegie Hall seemed veritably to vibrate when she unfurled the instrument, and one was awed by the fullness of the sound. Equally impressive was the way she spun out those long Verdi phrases, and the sentiment with which she imbued those phrases." –Thor Eckert Jr., *The Christian Science Monitor*, June 23, 1984

"Voices of this size and quality come along once in a generation if that often—not even recordings can really suggest the amplitude and cutting power of this thrilling instrument when hurled into the spaces of a large hall." –Peter Davis, *New York Magazine*, May 28, 1984

 ## William Tell II - 1984

There was great excitement for our second *William Tell* because the renowned Piero Cappuccilli would sing the title role. Cappuccilli had one of the most beautiful baritone voices in the world, and had rarely sung in New York. He had amazing control, linking several phrases without taking a breath, and a most expressive way of singing. He was also easy to work with, professional, prepared, calm, very charming and never demanding of extra consideration.

Much of the interest in this opera centers on the tenor because of the multiple high C's and one C sharp which are written, not optional. Franco Bonisolli, our tenor, was quite the character. He arrived in New York wearing boots that had once belonged to Errol Flynn. He exhibited a lot of nervousness during the rehearsals, repeatedly complaining about the air conditioning at Carnegie Hall. We got to the point where we hired a guard to stand by the switch to make sure the air was off.

On the night of the performance, it rained heavily. Bonisolli ordered John Broom, our office manager, to go out to buy apples, not an easy task in the Carnegie Hall neighborhood. John finally returned with two apples. Bonisolli was frantic. Two were not enough. He wanted many more.

I could not believe my ears when during the performance, I heard the unmistakable whirr of the air conditioner. Bonisolli actually left the stage in a frenzy as I started the famous ballet music. It was difficult to concentrate on the great delicacy and charm of this passage as I wondered if Bonisolli would return, or if Chris Merritt, the understudy, was changing into his tails. He did return, and we continued with the magnificent second act. The third act brought us the stunning aria sung by William Tell, "Resta Immobile," where he counsels his son Jemmy to remain absolutely still as he shoots the apple off his head with his bow and arrow. Cappuccilli was so superb in the delivery of this aria that the audience erupted in a deafening applause with many shouts of "Bis!" (encore). Finally, Cappuccilli looked at me with a half smile and a twinkle in his eye, and with a single swipe of his hand, turned the page back to the beginning of the aria. OONY had its first Bis!

The fourth act brought us the big aria of Arnold, the tenor. It has a beautiful cantilena, and then the cabaletta which ascends repeatedly up to a high C, step by step in the cruelest fashion. It requires enormous stamina, and Bonisolli did it, receiving a nice applause at the end. One person shouted "Bis!" and Bonisolli wanted his. So we repeated the cabaletta and OONY had its second Bis! At the end of the performance, Bonisolli had a huge crowd outside his dressing room with stacks of his recordings to be signed. I could see that it would be a good fifteen minutes until he would arrive at the reception, so I assigned my daughter Liz to wait for him. She later described leading Bonisolli down the stairs to leave the theater. When they got to the stage level, he said, "Uno momento," walked out to the center of the dark stage, and sang another high C to the empty house. He returned and said, "Okay, we go."

with Franco Bonisolli and Piero Cappuccilli. photo by Liz Queler

Cappuccilli returned in 1986 to sing La Gioconda with Ghena Dimitrova and an evening of Verdi arias and duets two nights later, again with Dimitrova, as a benefit for OONY.

La Gioconda - 1986

with Diane Curry, Paul Plishka, Piero Cappucilli, Ghena Dimitrova, Alexandrina Milcheva, and Giorgio Lamberti

12 - OONY Through The '80s

Kelly and Massa Photography

By the 1980s, OONY had grown in stature and recognition. Our concerts had become "happenings," often making the annual top ten lists of NYC music critics. Tickets were hard to come by, and singers were anxious to be a part of our alternative opera world.

Our board of twenty-three passionate opera lovers met four times a year and encouraged the development of printed materials and events to further engage our audience. To that end, Joan Arno suggested we create a Guild, which Norma Litton chaired. Members were invited to attend "operalogues" prior to each concert. This series was a chance to get a sneak peek at the upcoming concert, with arias and duets sung by the wonderful understudies in our Young Artists Program. I would accompany on the piano and give details about the composer and the work. On occasion, we hired writers or musicologists to speak.

We also implemented a big annual fund-raiser, co-chaired for many years by Mary Belknap and Joan Sarnoff. These black-tie events were hosted in some of the beautiful clubs and foreign consulates on New York's Park Avenue. Our singers would join us for an evening of wine and hors d'oeuvres, grace us with an aria or two, and socialize with the patrons.

Another important addition was the OONY Newsletter, spearheaded by its editor Herb Frank, with photographer David Shustak. We published three times a year, highlighting upcoming concerts, operalogues, news, and events. Since so much of the repertoire we presented was unknown, newsletters often included a plot summary and/or historical information. We also began to print libretti of our operas with translations and synopses, a practice we continued until 2007 when they were replaced by supertitles. Libretti were mailed to ticket holders several weeks before the performances, and distributed again for free at the concerts.

Up until this point we had various part-time workers in the office. Sandra Barr, a soprano and wife of our chorus member Frank Barr, became my assistant. I couldn't possibly list all the gaps she filled. Suffice to say that she accompanied me to all rehearsals and performances, ready to do whatever I needed with the greatest of good will and cooperation. In 1986, we hired our first director of development, Yvonne Altman, and in 1987 Alix Barthelmes joined our staff as general manager. Their vibrant leadership was a significant asset and they remained with us for twenty years.

with Norma Litton, Liz Cole, Yvonne Altman and Alix Barthelmes.
photo by Liz Queler

As of 1988, our concerts were recorded by National Public Radio for broadcast. In 1993, thanks to the generosity of board member

Gerald Rupp through the Vidda Foundation, we added the annual Vidda Award Recital, a series spotlighting up and coming talent.

Through all of this, however, and essential to the OONY experience, was the personal touch. As the years passed, the OONY family grew to include singers, musicians, patrons, and members of the global opera community. We had potluck suppers a few days before every performance, and celebratory dinners afterward, where young singers, superstars, members of the orchestra, and patrons all mingled. We watched each other's children grow and rejoiced in making beautiful music.

13 - Sydney, Australia - 1985

I arrived in Sydney on January 6th, during their summer season, a time when the city was alive with the arts. Energized to explore my home for the next two months, I spent my first day touring the city with Adrian Slack, the stage director for Mozart's *Abduction from the Seraglio,* which was my show. Adrian and I took a walk to a park called the Domain where there was a jazz festival in progress, with thousands of people listening to the music. Adrian explained to me that the following week the opera company would be presenting *The Tales of Hoffman* for 120,000 people and that Joan Sutherland would be singing all four soprano roles.

Adrian and I also walked to the Sydney Opera House, which is absolutely breathtaking. The centerpiece of the city, it is built on a promontory over the water. The harbor can be viewed from three sides. On the flight over I read about the man-eating sharks that inhabit the water. Evidently, they stay at the bottom so they are not visible.

Sydney Opera House is really a misnomer, as it is three theaters in one building, much like The Kennedy Center. The concert hall is the largest of the three theaters, the opera house is smaller, and the theater is the smallest. As Adrian and I continued our walk, I stopped to buy some fruit. Upon my return to the hotel, I found waiting for me a lovely welcoming gift from the opera company—a basket of fruit!

The next day we started rehearsals, which took place in a small studio in the Opera House not far from the green room. I had requested to see each singer privately for an hour so I could get to know them and go over their music. It gave me an opportunity to make comments which might seem embarrassing if they were made in the presence of others. *The Abduction of the Seraglio* has several very difficult roles starting with the two women, Constanza and Blonde. Constanza has three extremely difficult arias, one of which is quite high and Blonde has the famous "Durch Seeligkeit," which includes three high E's. Belmonte, the tenor, also has several difficult arias, one of which is usually cut, but we planned to do all three. Belmonte and Constanza, one of the romantic pairs in the opera were, in fact, Amanda Thane and Glenn Winslade, a married couple.

The green room was large, with its own cafeteria-style food service that was used by everyone in the company. People came up and introduced themselves. It was a friendly environment to lounge or eat or watch television. There was even a bar for drinks.

The cast was very good. The buffo basso role of Osmin was sung by Noel Mangin, who had done this role numerous times. He was co-author of the translation we were using, and had recorded that translation with Yehudi Menuhin at the Bath Festival in England.

That evening was the opening of *Tosca* with my friend and colleague Eugene Kohn conducting, so I raced home after rehearsals and raced back for the performance. The role of Tosca was beautifully sung by Pilar Lorengar, and I was very happy to be there for Eugene's success.

Patrick Veitch, general manager of the Australian Opera, invited me to a reception following the performance. The gathering included the artists, members of the company, sponsors, and quite unusually, members of the press. We all mingled while looking out at the beautiful harbor, drinking champagne and eating tiny vegetable sandwiches. It was a joy to be working in such a positive environment. Everyone was so gracious and welcoming except for one member of the press, who when writing about foreign artists, maintained that the opportunities should be given to Australians. The artists in the company, however, were quite anxious to work with foreign directors and conductors in hope of broadening their opportunities. The administration was acutely aware of this and did their best to not only invite outsiders, but also to send as many of their musical staff and young singers as possible, to study abroad or visit the great opera centers of the world.

The first week was very busy. The English translation which was sent to me by the company didn't bear much resemblance to what we were actually singing. I had to listen, copy, and re-copy words into my score which contained only the original German. We had to make additional adjustments so that some of the really high notes would be on a comfortable vowel for each singer. This comfort varies from singer to singer. Some are comfortable on *ee*, some prefer *ah*. Most are comfortable on *aw* and *oh*, so it was a challenge to look for words which contained these vowels. A thesaurus would have helped!

Stanley and Liz both called to wish me a happy birthday on January 11th. It was wonderful to hear from them and very dear that they realized it was a day later and took the trouble to do the math! Adrian brought flowers to the rehearsal and a little bottle of Dewars in deference to the Dewars ad that featured me. At the end of the rehearsal, "Happy Birthday" was well sung indeed! Adrian and I went to lunch in a pub that day and per the custom, brought our own sandwiches. We polished off the Dewars and the bottle became a vase for my flowers.

That evening, Jennifer McGregor, the Blonde in our show, invited me to the opening of a play in a theater owned by one of her friends. The theater was called Off Broadway and the title of the play was "Conversations with a Faint-Hearted Feminist." It was an extraordinary one-woman show. I had read about the book in the *New York Times*, and had read a review of the play so it was quite interesting to see it. It was set in New Zealand and adjusted for Australian audiences, but I didn't see much difference between the life of a harried housewife with a corporate husband in New Zealand, Australia, or America.

The theater itself was interesting. It was a former church, very old and nicely designed, with a bar outside and a little yard to enjoy during the intermissions. There I met a number of people who said they had never seen a woman conductor before and were planning to come to my opening performance. In the opera company itself, however, there were two women who were conductors. They were repetiteurs with the company, which is another term for rehearsal pianist and musical coach. They did prompting and stage duty, similar to what I had done with NYCO.

Saturday night, January 12th, was the Australian Opera in the park, and I was there watching 120,000 people loving every moment of it. Joan Sutherland was extraordinary. Before the performance, a tent was set up with a lovely buffet for the company, sponsors, and VIPs. The prime minister and his wife were in attendance, just mingling with the crowd, no bodyguards in sight. Some people on their way to take seats on the large lawn, stopped and spoke to the prime minister, and others were taking his photograph and asking for his autograph. This was the fourth year that the Sydney Festival was held on the Domain and featured Joan Sutherland. She was a great lady, an Australian treasure. The audiences knew it and simply adored her.

About two weeks before opening night, my good friend Leigh Raben arrived. On a rare day off, we took a bus trip into the Blue Mountains, which gave me the opportunity to talk with lots of people. Overall, I found the Australians I met refreshing, and in general, more relaxed than their American counterparts; and *everyone* had been to the opera house. Sydney is a big melting pot, not unlike New York, and I felt a kinship with the people who lived there. Many came directly after WWII, survivors of concentration camps, people who had lost everything and everyone. They moved there to make a new life.

Opening night! When I arrived at the theater and entered my dressing room, graciously loaned to me by music director Richard

Bonynge, with its beautiful view of the water, there was a large oval table covered with flowers, wine, and champagne. There were also telegrams, letters, cards, and presents from all the wonderful people on the staff and in the cast. My spirits were high as I conducted the performance, the first in a series of eight.

Opening night   Koala Park.

One exciting event during my stay was the arrival of the *QE2*, which had been in Australia only a few times before. Simultaneously, the Concorde arrived from London and flew right up the harbor. Thousands of people came to see these momentous events. My taxi driver that morning informed me that an armored car had arrived with a million dollars in cash for the wealthy Americans on the luxury liner, as spending money for their two days in Australia!

I loved the wildlife in Australia. Leigh and I went to Koala Park to see the bears who eat eucalyptus leaves. These trees grow only in this part of the world. The bears are really adorable, not very large, and generally stoned on the eucalyptus leaves, so they are quite tame. The emus were roaming around the park as well, stealing potato chips right out of the bag in my hand. They were quite friendly, albeit arrogant looking, harmless, and about adult human height, so I found myself at eye level with them. The kangaroos we saw were not as large as we expected. We had to stoop quite low to pet them. The baby we saw in the pouch was in there head first with its feet sticking out!

Many of the stage people and musicians entertained Leigh and me at their homes and in restaurants. One home was dug into the side of a hill overlooking the Sydney harbor. Most of the flats were tiny. Some were studio garden apartments with only one big room divided up with a patio outside. One hostess had a large group of people over for a cookout, which they called a barbie.

Leigh and I had our own cookout at the Motor Inn where we were staying. It had a lovely pool area which was countrified. Hard to imagine we were in the city at all. Everyone brought something, and it turned out to be one of the best meals we had in Sydney. I can still taste the pavlova, a wonderful Australian dessert of whipped cream and meringue.

14 - Thrilling Voices

 **Aprile Millo**

Eve Queler is opera's best friend. She enriches the tapestry of New York's music scene with memorable concerts. Hers is an indispensable contribution. —Aprile Millo

photo by Liz Queler

Aprile Millo auditioned for me in 1984 and I immediately asked her to cover the soprano role in *William Tell*. The covers did a performance with the orchestra at Lehman College several days before the opening at Carnegie Hall. This performance had great significance for me and OONY. It marked the beginning of a long and wonderful relationship with Aprile, and two members of our orchestra announced their engagement on this very night! This was the third or fourth couple who met at Opera Orchestra and married. We were becoming even more of a family.

Aprile was a member of the Lindemann Young Artist Program at the Met, so many people had already heard her beautiful voice. She gave a stunning performance. In one of the large ensembles, she interpolated a high E flat. It was unexpected and very exciting. Aprile always had the measure of a piece, where its climaxes would be, and how she could make it dramatically and vocally

(L) with Matteo Manuguerra, Aprile Millo, Kristján Jóhannson and Stella Zambalis
(R) with Aprile Millo and Licia Albanese.
photo by Liz Queler

exciting. Her phrasing was exquisite, and her vocalisms in the Italian language extremely impressive and beautiful.

After this performance, I invited her to sing with OONY each year for the next five years. We did memorable performances of *I Lombardi, La Battaglia di Legnano, Andrea Chénier, Il Pirata* (covered by Renée Fleming), and *La Wally.* The last four operas I did with Aprile were semi-staged by Ira Siff, giving these works a strong dramatic impact but also one with sensitivity. For Aprile, the music and words were all one. Soon she launched a great career in New York, and her performances sold out very quickly.

 **Leonie Rysanek**

It had become the norm for people to send me unusual works to consider, and I spent many hours sifting through cassettes. This is how I was first introduced to *Dalibor.* I became smitten by Smetana! Thanks in no small part to my dear friend Yveta Synek Graff, wife of longtime OONY board member Malcolm Graff, I spent many wonderful musical years exploring the Czech repertoire.

Yveta left her native Czechoslovakia while still a child and moved with her parents to Paris, where her father was a diplomat. Speaking both Czech and French fluently, she was invaluable to me as a language coach, and she became quite an asset in the opera community. The foremost translator of Czech opera, Yveta was a tireless advocate for Czech music in the United States. Her efforts reaped beautiful translations of several Czech operas commissioned and or adopted by the Met, The Seattle Opera, and the New York Philharmonic.

Fans still write telling me about their favorites among my concerts, with many mentioning Janáček's *Jenůfa*. The exquisite singing of Gabriela Beňačková coupled with the searing dramatic performance of Leonie Rysanek and the gorgeous music of Janáček, enveloped the audience and all of us on the stage that evening in 1988.

I first met Leonie in Australia, where she was singing *Jenůfa* in English. We became friendly, and I invited her to repeat the role in New York, this time in the original Czech language, a first for her. Leonie was not only a fine singer with many colors to her voice, but she was also a powerful and seasoned actor. She captivated our audience with her regal stature. At one point, as she was crossing

with Leonie Rysanek
photo by Liz Queler

the stage in front of me, I noticed with alarm that her chair had been removed by an uninformed stagehand. For this concert, I had engaged a prompter, who was seated by my podium. While I was conducting, I tapped him gently on the head with my baton and whispered to him to give Leonie his chair. Without breaking character, she said quietly, "It is all right. I will be fine."

While the entire evening was electric, there was a particularly unusual and devastating portion of the story that undoubtedly stood out in the memories of our audience.

Jenůfa is a love story of tangled relationships in a small village. The ingenue, our soprano Jenůfa (Gabriela Beňačková), spurned by her lover and pregnant with his child, is locked away to have her baby in secret. Then the story takes a turn. Her stepmother Kostelnička (Leonie Rysanek), fearful that Jenůfa will end up alone and disgraced, concludes that there is only one solution. At the end of Act II, while Jenůfa sleeps, Kostelnička takes the baby to a stream and with excruciating sorrow, drowns it. Leonie's intense delivery of this brutal aria, culminating in an anguished cry, provided one of the greatest dramatic moments in opera I've had the privilege to experience. No one present will ever forget that final wail. The roar of applause and the standing ovation lasted the entirety of the second intermission.

with Yveta Graff, Leonie Rysanek, and Gabriela Beňačková

 **Renée Fleming**

Eve Queler introduced me to the art of bel canto style. I have always been grateful for the amount of time she spent with me as a young developing singer. She encouraged me to strive for greater heights both vocally and musically. I believe she singlehandedly enabled me to continue singing this repertoire. Eve's personal style is such a joy. She ignites her forces with a real collaborative feeling, which isn't often experienced between singers and orchestra. I have always felt nurtured in an Opera Orchestra engagement, which is one of the reasons why I so eagerly return as often as I am invited.
—Renée Fleming

with Renée Fleming and Brian Nedvin. Photo © Steve J. Sherman

I first heard Renée Fleming when I was a judge for the Musician's Emergency Fund competition for young singers. Part of her reward for winning was to sing at Alice Tully Hall. At this concert, she sang the final aria from Bellini's *La Sonnambula*. I immediately invited her to cover Aprile Millo in another Bellini opera, *Il Pirata*. For this concert, there was an understudy performance with orchestra in New Jersey which was attended by Aprile, who was full of gracious admiration for Renée.

The following season we did *La Sonnambula* at Carnegie Hall with June Anderson. I invited Renée to cover June in the title role. One day we were rehearsing *La Sonnambula* with piano at my apartment when my son, Andy, came in with his three-month-old son, Sam. Renée picked up Sam and exclaimed, "Oh, I want one!" A year later when her first daughter was born, I was summoned to the hospital. Upon arrival, I was instructed to put on a gown and head cover. Then Renée handed me the baby, immediately produced a camera from under the covers, and took a photo of me in my "whites" holding the baby.

After the two performances Renée covered, there was no question in my mind that I would present her at Carnegie Hall. The first opera she sang with us was the rarely heard *La Dame Blanche* by Boieldieu. This was a charming story of a woman who pretends to be a ghost to clear up an inheritance question, and of course be reunited with her sweetheart. Renée had two outfits she wore, one for the character Anna, and the other for the ghost. She could change in an instant with a cleverly designed coat.

The opera had some funny moments. In the scene which decides the outcome of a trial, we needed a lit candle. The decision would be pronounced when the candle went out. All the props were ready, but the fire department would not allow an open flame, so our baritone found a battery-powered candle. Of course, we had a lot of fun with this whole thing. Renée not only played the part with

photo © Beth Bergman 2012

humor in this concert version, but often with embellishments. Her experience singing in nightclubs was very good training.

The season after *La Dame Blanche* (1992–1993), Renée returned in another Bellini opera, *La Straniera*. The following season, I went to the San Francisco Opera to hear her sing the role of Salome opposite

Plácido Domingo in Massenet's *Hérodiade*. Renée wanted to explore more adventurous styles and was wonderful in all of them. I knew I had to have this in New York. We presented it with Grace Bumbry singing the title role, and Renée singing Salome.

50th Anniversary Gala, Carnegie Hall. With Dolora Zajick, Bryan Hymel, Renée Fleming, Marcello Giordani, and Krassimira Stoyanova
Photo © Steve J. Sherman

One day I had a call from Renée's manager at the time, Merle Hubbard, asking my advice about Renée singing the title role of Rossini's *Armida* at the Pesaro Festival in Italy. I told him I only knew one aria, a set of variations in Act II which I had performed with Renata Scotto. I was sure Renée could sing it, but was not familiar with the rest of the opera. On my advice, Renée accepted the role and I went to Pesaro to hear her. It was stunning. The following season (1996), we did *Armida* for Renée. This opera is unique in that it has seven different tenor roles. It was a very big project to cast and produce. In all, we presented eight concerts with Renée, culminating in Donizetti's beautiful *Lucrezia Borgia*. Renée was consistently brilliant, warm-hearted, and gracious. Several seasons later, the Met mounted a production of *Armida* for Renée, as well as a production of *Il Pirata*. At that point, we were responsible for a number of operas later produced by the Met, including *Khovanshchina* as well as all of the Czech operas in the Czech language, which we were the first to do in New York and sometimes in the United States.

Dmitri Hvorostovsky

It is always a pleasure to perform with Eve, whose professionalism and enthusiasm are an incredible example for the whole music world.
—Dmitri Hvorostovsky

photo by Liz Queler

There was an advertisement in the *New York Times* for a concert of young artists from the Bolshoi, featuring Madame Irina Arkhipova at Symphony Space. I had heard Arkhipova sing the role of Azucena in Verdi's *Il Trovatore* in Szeged, Hungary, during the time I was there recording. I thought she was wonderful. She had a fantastic rich voice, especially in the lower range. She began the famous aria softer than I had ever heard it. This was in an outdoor performance in a churchyard, and we heard every note, even her whisper. I was very anxious to hear her again as she did not come to the United States often.

I attended the concert and heard for the first time the twenty-seven-year-old Dmitri Hvorostovsky sing the aria "Per me giunto" from Verdi's *Don Carlo*. How to explain the stunning effect Dmitri Hvorostovsky had on me? Initially, I was struck by his extraordinary good looks, but when he opened his mouth, my adoration transferred to his exquisite sound. Dmitri phrased the beautiful aria in long, expressive lines, demonstrating amazing breath control. I had only heard one other singer phrase that aria in a similar fashion, my old friend Piero Cappuccilli.

He sang another piece at that concert, an a capella song in Russian which he announced as having the name Noc, which I understood to mean "night." Several people at that concert asked me if he would be singing with me. I sure hoped he would.

That evening I joined the singers from the concert at the Russian Tea Room for a reception. I invited them to the OONY office the next day, and we got to know each other a little better. I was planning Tchaikovsky's *Maid of Orleans* for the next season, and I invited several of them to participate although there was nothing for Dmitri, as I had already cast the leading baritone. However, this was the start of a happy working relationship with him. The next month, he won the top prize at the Singer of the World Competition in Wales.

It took some time for me to find opera repertoire which was suitable for him but while we were searching for the right opera, we were able to present him in recital on two different occasions. The first was in Alice Tully Hall. By this time,

with Olga Borodina and Dmitri Hvorostovsky
photo by Alix Barthelmes

people had begun to hear about him, and we sold out the hall. One year later, we were able to present him in Carnegie Hall, also selling out. Each of these concerts wiped out our deficit for the season.

OONY then presented him with orchestra in a concert of arias and duets in Carnegie Hall with the mezzo-soprano Olga Borodina.

Happily, I was able to find two operas in the bel canto style for him. The first was Verdi's *I Masnadieri,* which Dmitri first sang in London. The next was Donizetti's beautiful *La Favorita*, in a cast with Jennifer Larmore.

I always loved working with Dmitri. I loved his voice and his sincerity, which always touched my heart. Sometimes he sounded like he was crying when he sang. I feel very fortunate that I attended that half-empty concert at Symphony Space which gave us Dmitri.

with June LeBell and
Dmitri Hvorostovksy

La Favorita - 2001

with Jennifer Larmore, Gregory Kunde, Dmitri Hvorostovsky,
Vitalij Kowaljow, Angela Gilbert, and Barton Green.

15 - Kirov Opera - 1993

For my 1992–93 season, I decided to do Tchaikovsky's *Mazeppa,* featuring June Anderson. OONY was presenting two bel canto operas that season, one Bellini and one Donizetti, so it was a nice change in style. Russian opera was a big challenge for me because I had never studied the language. Most of the operas I had done were in Italian, French, or German—languages I speak. I invited Sergei Leiferkus, Gegam Grigorian, and Paul Plishka, all of whom were fluent in Russian, to complete the cast.

When Valery Gergiev learned that I would be presenting *Mazeppa* in Carnegie Hall, he invited me to conduct the work several weeks earlier in a staged production at the Kirov Opera, in the Mariinsky Theatre in St. Petersburg, Russia. Grigorian needed to learn the role, and Maestro Gergiev assured me he would personally coach him. My daughter Liz, who had accompanied me several times to France, Prague, and Italy, was my companion on this trip. We were both very excited for our first trip to Russia.

There were very few stores near our hotel, and the ones we found were sparsely stocked. There was an international store which only accepted US dollars, where we could buy items like tissues and bottled water. Breakfast at the hotel was limited. There would be coffee but no milk, or coffee but no sugar, and very little in the way of eggs or cheese, but lots of rich cakes.

The Kirov seemed enormous to me, and I got lost more than once. We never rehearsed in the theater as the ballet had the stage during the afternoons. At night, the opera played, and we went to the performances. My rehearsals took place in a room unlike any I had ever worked in before, with an actual stage and pit. However, due to the shape of the pit, the orchestra sat in a slightly different configuration from how they would sit for the performance.

One day, we went on a sightseeing trip to the river where we saw a bear on a leash! We alighted from the car and walked to the St. Peter and Paul Fortress, the burial site of the Russian czars. On our way out of the cathedral, we were accosted by a group of boys trying to sell us T-shirts. They swarmed all over us. We finally shooed them away and proceeded back to the car, passing a young man on the street who opened up a music stand and began to sing of all things, the Schubert Ständchen. I reached for my wallet to give him a ruble. No wallet! Liz immediately realized what had happened and took off after the boys, who were rollicking and laughing, but they got away. My wallet contained my passport, exit visa, credit card, and all my rubles. My dollars were safe inside a money belt. We returned to the car and explained to our driver, what had happened. He ran off, leaving Liz and me in the car. When he returned, he told us the police had caught two of the boys and drove us to identify them. We arrived at what seemed to be a subway station and were led downstairs to a holding pen. The two boys were in a little cage, and I did recognize them, particularly one of them who had been very close to me with a pitiful expression on his face, begging me to buy one of the shirts.

"Mrs. Queler, if we could have your valuables returned to you, would you agree not to press charges?" My first thought was that I couldn't possibly do that. The boys were stealing. As I hesitated, Liz reminded me that I needed my paperwork, so I relented. We got back in the car with one of the boys, who directed us to a deserted alley near the river. He got out to retrieve my valuables, which were hidden in between the stones of a wall under a staircase. He said he had thrown the wallet in the river and that my passport was somewhere else, and he would bring it to me later. I got back some items, but of course, not the money.

As we drove back to the police station, our driver told the boy that I was a very famous conductor from New York, and that he didn't want us to take a bad impression back home to

America. The boy said he was not actually the thief, but the one who distracted the victim so the thief could do the stealing. He said he worked for a gang and he that he was addicted to drugs and showed us the needle marks on his arm. He promised to bring my passport the the theater later that day.

That evening, Liz and I went to a concert she was eager to hear, and when we returned to the hotel, my wallet was sitting at the front desk. Someone had found it and brought it to the hotel since it had my room card in it. There was a note from the person who returned it, with his phone number. I asked the desk clerk to call this person and invite him to my performance. At that moment, the boy showed up with my passport. He said that he was now in trouble with his gang, and had to leave town and was going to his grandmother's house. He showed me the train ticket. By this time, I knew his name. I kissed him goodbye and wished him well.

The next day was another rehearsal and a trip to the Hermitage Museum, a breathtaking place. We were not permitted to take any photographs, but I spent some time studying the huge mural of the Battle of Poltava, which takes place in the opera.

Finally came the night of the performance, and I had never even seen the scenery. Arriving at the theater, I went to the dressing rooms to see the singers in their costumes and wigs, so I could tell who was who. When I was called to the podium, I entered the orchestra pit for the first time. I had only a few moments to find the oboes, who were not where I expected them to be!

The third act opens with a big symphonic piece introducing the Battle of Poltava. Imagine that in front of me, I suddenly saw the exact same mural I had studied the day before at the Hermitage. It was even larger than the original, covering the entire curtain. In front of the mural was a brass band, trumpets and trombones in brilliant parade costumes stretching across the stage. It was one of the most exciting things I had ever experienced and all a big surprise. Well, I thought, what a debut! You never know what to expect. It took every ounce of self-control to calm myself down to begin the next scene very quietly with murmuring celli.

After the performance, waiting to greet me backstage were the people who had found my wallet. They were young engineering students who brought me the largest box of chocolates I had ever seen.

with Valery Gergiev and Gegam Gregorian. photo by Liz Queler

To celebrate, we were invited to the house of the tenor. Liz and I waited for Maestro Gergiev, and we all went together.

Gegam Grigorian triumphantly served the feast he had prepared. The food, vodka, and toasts were endless. No one asked what the meat was. We had been drinking a sufficient amount of vodka not to care. Maestro Gergiev drank a toast to me saying I was the first American to conduct at the Kirov, and he hoped the first of many. Another time he raised his glass to me and said, "To all mothers." Liz drank with enthusiasm to that one! It all felt like a scene from a movie.

Mazeppa, NYC

with Gegam Grigorian, Sergei Leiferkus, Paul Plishka, June Anderson,
Frank Barr, Paul Groves, Eugenie Grunewald and Martin Dillon.
photo by Alix Barthelmes

with June Anderson. photo by Liz Queler

16 - Hamburg Opera - 1994

In a note from baritone Renato Capecchi, we have been instructed that in Italian the word maestra *can only mean schoolmistress, and that all conductors should be called* maestro, *regardless of gender.*
—*OONY Newsletter*, Winter 1994

On opening night, during the second intermission, there was a knock at my dressing room door. An attractive, nicely dressed man asked, "Wo is dein Mann?" (Where is your husband?) I answered, "Mein Mann ist nicht hier." (My husband is not here.) He seemed confused and continued to look inside my dressing room. Suddenly, I realized that he had come to pay me for conducting the performance and was expecting to see a man. It was customary at that time to pay cash to guest performers at the second intermission. I said, "Ich bin Die Dirigentin." (I am the conductor.) He was shocked but recovered quickly and looked at the sign on my door which said Eve Queler, Dirigentin. He was embarrassed, and we both had a good laugh. After much "Entschuldigen" (Pardon me), I was paid. Each subsequent performance brought much laughter during the second intermission as he handed me my money.

Earlier in my stint there, I had a somewhat different experience navigating the confusion around my title, gender, and position, when I was introduced to the general music director of the Hamburg Opera, Gerd Albrecht. A very nice lady who ran the office explained to him that I would be conducting *Don Pasquale*. He glared at me and said, "Das soll nicht sein" (That should not be), turned his back, and walked away. It struck us funny and we both burst out laughing.

17 - Bob Wilson - Tristan and Isolde - 1997

with Robert Breault, Heikki Siukola, Greg Ryerson,
Elizabeth Connell, Petra Lang, and Joel Sorenson
photo by Alix Barthelmes

Bob Wilson, board member of OONY and a patron of NYCO, was a financier. Bob loved Wagner, liked Bellini, but not so much Donizetti. In 1978, some years before I met Bob, I had conducted my first *Tristan and Isolde* at the University of Maryland in a summer workshop for orchestra players. This performance was so successful that I brought this group to Carnegie Hall to perform it on New Year's Eve the same year. The performance was taped and I gave a copy to Bob, who then suggested that I present *Tristan* with Opera Orchestra in our subscription series. He felt that my interpretation of the opera was from the viewpoint of Isolde rather than that of Tristan, which in his opinion, was the version usually heard.

Tristan and Isolde was certainly not the unusual or obscure repertoire which OONY generally presented, but I noted that it had not been done by the Met in fifteen years, and I decided that a masterpiece could be repeated every fifteen years. Besides, my passionate love for this opera prevented me from finding any reasons why we could not or should not do it.

Presenting *Tristan* was a more expensive project for OONY, due to the necessary increase in size of the orchestra and the length of the opera (5 hours!), requiring more rehearsal time. We also had to pay Carnegie Hall quite a bit in overtime fees. Bob worked out a financial agreement with the business manager of OONY, promising to cover any shortfall himself. In the end, it turned out that the performance was totally sold out and a huge success. We were able to make a recording, thanks to a special agreement with the musicians union and Carnegie Hall. The performance took place on Sunday, February 9, 1997 at 1pm. By 7pm, we were at dinner with 200 thrilled patrons and board members! That same season, Bob traveled to Frankfurt to attend my debut there with a concert performance of *Tancredi* by Rossini.

I remember some wonderful times Stanley and I spent with him at our home in the Berkshires. Bob and Stanley shared many hours talking about philosophy and the investment world.

I did a few more Bellini operas after *Tristan*, which helped me hold on to Bob a bit longer, but we did not see him very often. When he heard Stanley had entered an assisted living facility, he wrote me a beautiful note about his memory of their conversations and he commented, "These are not our best years." I answered his note but never heard from him again.

In 2013, after giving away his 800 million dollars, Bob jumped off his 16th floor terrace of the San Remo.

18 - A Great Italian Tenor

It has always been a pleasure to be on the stage with Eve. Everything is under control, and it is a real delight to sing in the magic of the atmosphere created by her.
—Carlo Bergonzi

with Renata Scotto, Vicente Sardinero, Mark Munkittrick, Gwendolyn Killebrew, and Carlo Bergonzi.   photo by Jean Laurain

My musical life was so greatly enriched by meeting and working with Carlo Bergonzi. What an open, smiling, cooperative individual he was. His great voice was a part of his personality, always "up." The first time we worked together was in 1977, when he sang the title role in Puccini's *Edgar* opposite Renata Scotto. That performance was recorded live by CBS. Our next concert together was Verdi's *I Due Foscari* with Margarita Castro-Alberti and Renato Bruson in 1981. A few years later came Verdi's *I Lombardi*, which would be the first big concert starring Aprile Millo, with Paul Plishka repeating the role he had sung in 1972. After Carnegie Hall, we took this production to the Academy of Music in Philadelphia. At rehearsals, I often combined the cover cast with the superstars. Carlo loved working with the young singers and was particularly generous in sharing words of wisdom.

We presented Carlo in a recital at Carnegie Hall accompanied by Vincenzo Scalera on two occasions, one in April 1994 and again in April 1996. To celebrate the occasion, Robert Wagenfield, an OONY board member, threw a splendid dinner for Bergonzi at the Columbus Club in New York City.

with Robert Wagenfeld, Renata Scotto, Carlo Bergonzi,
Licia Albanese, and Aprile Millo. photo by David Shustak

We made one more attempt to work together. I offered Carlo a concert of arias featuring the final scene of *Otello*, which I had previously heard him sing so movingly as a guest artist at a concert featuring the winners of the Licia Albanese Puccini competition. To my surprise, Carlo responded that he wanted to do the entire opera. I encouraged him to do excerpts instead, but he was adamant. My board was quite nervous about Carlo attempting the role for the first time at age seventy-five. There was also the issue of producing an opera already in regular repertoire at the Met, a practice OONY tried to avoid. All the same, we forged ahead.

This would be my first *Otello*. Fortunately, I was invited to conduct several performances of it in Toluca, Mexico, several months prior.

Rehearsals were not going well. Carlo was struggling. On the night of the performance, he was not in good voice. There was huge pressure as it was a sold-out house. In Box 1 were his colleagues— Domingo, Pavarotti, and Carreras—who had all come to honor the great tenor. Carlo tried valiantly and sang the first two acts, then had to bow out. I was told when he left the stage he said, "Son finito."

Nothing however, can erase the memory of that great voice and personality which live on in his recordings and in our hearts.

19 - Buenos Aires - Elizabetta, regina d'Inghilterra - 2004

Eve Queler was one of the first people to welcome me back to America with open arms after eight years in Europe. I believe her trust and confidence opened the door to my American career. For that I will always be grateful to this wonderful lady.
—Jennifer Larmore

with Jennifer in costume at the Teatro Colon.

It sounds like it could be a bel canto opera. It could be and it is! This "Elisabetta" is the ferocious Queen Elisabetta Regina d'Inghilterra, the same name as the elegant hotel in Rome. This *Elisabetta,* written by Rossini in 1815, and I both made our debuts at the Teatro Colon in Buenos Aires, Argentina, on October 19, 2004.

The title role was magnificently sung by Jennifer Larmore, who had already recorded it in London. *Elisabetta* was the first of nine operas which Rossini wrote for the Teatro San Carlo in Naples. Each opera had an extraordinary role for the great Spanish soprano Isabella Colbran. They also contained unusually difficult roles for the leading tenors. The fiery coloratura role of Elisabetta is technically very difficult, really requiring more than one voice—true mezzo color in the middle and lower register, and a secure, easy top, with numerous B flats and even some C's. It also requires an actress who can portray a young girl in love as well as a betrayed queen. Ms. Larmore did not disappoint on any level. She gave a brilliant performance and looked stunning in a production designed by Claudio Hanczye, staged by Marc Verzatt, with beautiful costumes by Eduardo Caldirola, some of which weighed forty pounds! The original Elisabetta would have envied her interpreter. The other singers of the cast were members of the Teatro Colon, and in at least one performance, I had three tenors all named Carlos. I had to be careful with my written memos!

Everyone was extremely congenial, not only people with whom I worked, but the warm public as well. The October Festival was underway, and the streets were lively with beautifully costumed tango dancers.

I fell in love with the Teatro Colon from the very first moment I saw it. This magnificent building—beautiful, elegant, aristocratic, and comfortable—had phenomenal acoustics, possibly the best in the world. Its history, displayed on posters throughout the halls, encompassed the greatest names in opera.

The Colon became like a home to me. Aside from my hotel and occasional restaurants, I spent all my time there. A big difference between the Colon and many other theaters in which I have worked is the backstage area. The marble staircases and iron banisters were exactly the same as they were in the outer lobbies of the theater. A great credit to the Argentine people is that in spite of the economic depression at that time, they still kept the theater in good repair. It was filled to capacity at every performance.

In addition to the six performances I conducted of *Elisabetta Regina* over the course of three weeks, there was a lot of other activity on the stage. While I was there, the BBC Orchestra played two performances and there was a Martha Argerich piano festival. With a capacity of 4,000 (including standing room), the Colon is the only large concert hall in Buenos Aires, so it is always booked. The Colon is huge, with 1,200 employees. The theater extends well under the Avenue de 9 Julio, a superhighway the guidebooks claim is as wide as two football fields. I had to cross this avenue each time I went to the theater. It required several lights to cross. The designers of the theater really valued the people who would be working there, and showed it by providing them an entrance equally aesthetically attractive as that used by the public. Artists usually sneak in some side door. Under the Avenue de 9 Julio are three giant floors of sub-basement, which house the construction shops, storage for scenery, wigs, costumes, and shoes, as well as offices and a restaurant. One particular section of the theater interested me. On the left side of the house, there are side boxes that are covered, making it impossible to see who is seated within. When I inquired, I was told that these boxes were reserved for widows.

The new director of the theater at the time was Tito Capobianco, with whom I had worked when I was a pianist at NYCO. It was wonderful to see him again after so many years, still handsome and charming.

Jennifer Larmore, who comes from Atlanta, made her American debut with me and OONY in Bellini's *I Capuleti ed I Montecchi* in 1994. It was a memorable performance which also starred Mariella Devia as Giulietta. That year, Jennie was also the winner of the Richard Tucker award. I engaged her again in 2001 to perform in Donizetti's *La Favorita,* singing the title role opposite Dmitri Hvorostovsky. When she was invited to sing the title role in Rossini's *Elisabetta Regina* at Teatro Colon, she requested that I be the conductor.

We became very close during the wonderful six weeks we spent in Buenos Aires. We often traveled together to and from the theater. Whenever our car stopped for a red light, a beggar, usually a young man on a bicycle, would stop outside our car window, and Jennie would always give him something. She could never turn down a beggar, a result she believed, of her background as a daughter of missionaries. It was always a delight for me to work with her. The role of Elisabetta could go very high for a mezzo, but the final scene in E major gave no problem for Jennie, who executed the high B's with ease. She had an excellent, totally accurate coloratura, and even added a high C in one of her cadenzas.

In 2008, we did another performance together when she sang the role of Tigrana in Puccini's *Edgar* opposite Marcello Giordani. Whether she played a lad like Romeo, a queen like Elisabetta, or the rejected temptress Tigrana in *Edgar*, she became that character, even in concert.

20 - William Tell III - 2005

photo by Liz Queler

Marcello Giordani had come to me when I was casting for Donizetti's *Lucrezia Borgia* with Renée Fleming in the title role. Marcello had sung this opera with Renée at La Scala, and she wanted to sing it with him in New York. His participation in that concert on Valentine's Day, February 14, 2000, would commence a decade of enjoyable collaboration.

The next season in 2001, I did Meyerbeer's spectacular *Les Huguenots* for Marcello. I am a Meyerbeer enthusiast and up until that year I had done his other operas, *L'Africaine* and *Robert Le Diable*, but I had to wait until I found a tenor with a secure, brilliant C sharp to perform *Les Huguenots*. High C is considered the top note in the tenor voice. Most composers who wrote a high C in a tenor aria would write only one, as in Puccini's beautiful "Che gelida manina," from *La Boheme*. Most often, composers would write a C sharp in the middle of an embellishment to be tapped without being held. *Les Huguenots* demands the note to be sung and held without any accompaniment. Marcello's performance was flawless.

Each time I have done *William Tell* has been because I found a tenor with the necessary high notes to sing the role. It was my pleasure to resurrect this opera for Marcello in 2005. Although the title character of the opera is a baritone, the most spectacular vocal writing is for the tenor. The high C sharp, which occurs in the second act in the middle of a trio for three men, was executed with ease. A far more grueling and exposed section for the tenor arrives in his Act 4 aria. This aria is in C major, which means the climactic note will be a high C. But in this aria, there are eight of them if you do all of the repeats. They are particularly difficult to sing because they were written with a slow ascent up to the C, requiring huge stamina, somewhat more difficult than the high C in *La Boheme*. Clearly, Rossini had a tenor who could sing this or he would not have written it this way. When I do operas that were written for a particular person, this is my challenge: to find a voice with a similar color and range as the long gone singer for whom the piece was written. Marcello Giordani was this singer.

After the aria, our performance was literally stopped by a prolonged ovation. I knew it would be a few minutes and stepped off the podium to sit for a moment in one of the chairs in front of me which had been set for the singers. After acknowledging his ovation, Marcello came over to me and pulled me off the chair, saying, "We are going to do it again!" I said, "Are you crazy?" thinking that we might go into overtime. He said, "Only the cabaletta," the second part of the aria which is the fast section. As we began, I suddenly thought to myself, I wish Marcello would move to the other side of the stage so that the audience on that side would get a closer look at him. Unbelievably, he seemed to read my mind, and darted across the stage, shook his fist at the chorus who were urging him on to the fight, and turned to finish the aria. There followed another prolonged ovation.

In 2007, OONY experienced a major alteration. Several of our most active board members had passed away and several more were not well. Our board shrank and Alix, Yvonne, and I were offered retirement packages. Alix and Yvonne accepted, but I declined. I thought we still had some important concerts to present and some great young talent to spotlight. Quite simply, I wasn't done yet.

We hired Deborah Surdi as executive director. Debbie came to us after twenty-eight years with RCA Red Seal and Sony Classical Records. She was not only a business executive but also a singer who had sung all the major soprano roles with the Amato Opera. Debbie had attended many of our performances and loved what we did. Her enthusiasm, knowledge, and wonderful sense of humor have been a great asset to OONY and me.

In 2008, Marcello Giordani was a major figure, along with Renée Fleming in creating a gala for me and OONY on the occasion of our 100th performance at Carnegie Hall. Incredibly, we had amassed that many performances! Renata Scotto was the master of ceremonies for the event. A wonderful group of singers performed, including Dolora Zajick, Krassimira Stoyanova, Aprile Millo, Eglise Gutiérrez, Daniel Mobbs, Steven Gaertner, and Bryan Hymel, who stepped in at the last minute to make his Carnegie Hall debut replacing Stephen Costello, who was ill. One month later, Marcello sang with us again, this time the title role in Puccini's *Edgar* with Latonia Moore, Jennifer Larmore, and Stephen Gaertner.

with Giovanni Guagliardo, Jennifer Larmore, Marcello Giordani, Latonia Moore, and Stephen Gaertner.

21 - More Beautiful Voices

With all the talk of tenors and high C's, I don't want to neglect some of the great low F's.

L'Amore di Tre Re - 2006

with Sam Ramey, Gaston Rivero, Pavel Baransky,
Fernando de la Mora, and Fabiana Bravo. photo by Alix Barthelmes

Sam Ramey began with OONY as a young artist in the late 1960s as Monterone in *Rigoletto* at Alice Tully Hall. He also appeared in the title role of *The Marriage of Figaro* when I conducted at NYCO. He grew into a star, and sang with us several times at Carnegie Hall, most notably in Verdi's *Attila* and Meyerbeer's *Robert le Diable*. There was never a more gracious, willing, and helpful colleague.

When it comes to basses, however, no one can challenge Paul Plishka for the number of times he sang with me, and always so beautifully. The first was Verdi's *I Lombardi* in 1972 with Renata Scotto and José Carreras. At that time, Paul was a young singer doing supporting roles at the Met. That would soon change as he grew into all the leading bass roles. Paul sang no less than twenty-three operas with us. Paul's voice was so rich and full. His languages were always excellent, whether the opera was French, Italian, Russian, or Czech. When he sang with me, I always felt I had a friend on stage.

I Masnadieri - 1999

with Christopher Pucci, Brian Nedvin, Antonio Nagore, Sally Wolf, Paul Plishka, Julian Konstantinov, and Dmitri Hvorostovsky. photo by Alix Barthelmes

Baritone Matteo Manuguerra came to me recommended by Richard Tucker. I liked Matteo and his voice so much that I offered him as many roles as he had time to accept. We worked together for the next eighteen years.

Lucrezia Borgia in 2000 was my introduction to Stephanie Blythe. Stephanie's voice completely bowled me over. To describe it, one critic said, "Stephanie doesn't sing Fricka, she *is* Fricka." She has a warm, wonderful, big sound and is a joy to work with. I couldn't wait to offer her the role of Malcolm in Rossini's *La Donna del Lago* and the title role in *Mignon*. Fortunately, she accepted both of these offers, much to my pleasure and that of the audience.

Lucrezia Borgia - 2000

(L to R) with Charles Robert Stephens, Michael Corvino, Justin Vickers, Marcello Giordani, Renée Fleming, Luiz-Ottavio Faria, Christopher Mooney, Stephanie Blythe, Dean Peterson, Martin Dillon, and Brian Nedvin. photo by Alix Barthelmes

At the turn of the new century, a number of singers emerged with exceptionally beautiful voices with whom I was eager to work. As I have previously mentioned, I like to begin with new singers by engaging them as understudies for a big role. That way, I can get to know them well so we can work comfortably together, and they will be able to perform at their best.

I first engaged Latonia Moore to cover the leading soprano role in Bizet's *Pearl Fishers* and von Weber's *Der Freischütz*. There were other concerts with piano before I offered her the leading soprano role in Cilea's *L'Arlesiana* in Carnegie Hall. The last opera we did together was Puccini's *Edgar* in 2008. One Saturday a few years ago, I was listening to the Met broadcast of *Aida*. I missed the beginning so I did not hear the announcements, but immediately recognized the gorgeous voice of Latonia. This was in fact her Met debut, stepping in at the last minute, no less! I was so thrilled for her.

L'Arlesiana - 2007

(L to R) with Giuseppe Filianoti, John Daly Goodwin, Latonia
Moore, Colette Boudreaux, Mark Risinger, Weston Hurt, Ihn Kyu
Lee, and Marianna Cornetti. photo by Alix Barthelmes

In the ensuing years, I was delighted to nurture the wonderful
vocal talents of Francisco Casanova, Ellie Dehn, Taylor Stayton, Eric
Owens, and many more young singers who appear in the following
pages of photos of our casts.

La Battaglia di Legnano - 2002

with Krassimir Stoyanova, Francisco Casanova, Carla Wood,
Vitalij Kowaljow, Carlo Guelfi, Timothy Lafontaine, Gregory Keil,
Frank Barr, Jason Grant, and Matthew Walley.
photo by Alix Barthelmes

Eglise Gutiérrez has a rich, lush voice that can go all the way to high E. The first opera she did with me was *Mignon* with Stephanie Blythe singing the title role. Soon after that, I presented her in *Lakmé* in the title role, which made great use of her high E's. Later she sang the title role in *La Sonnambula* with OONY in Carnegie Hall, with Ferrucio Furlanetto singing Rodolfo.

with Renata Scotto and Eglise Gutiérrez

One of my main missions has always been to match new singers with seasoned artists. Ferrucio had a magnificent command of his instrument. When his voice descended to the low G at the end of his aria, it seemed that time stood still, as I felt I could actually touch the tone. At one point, I overheard him saying to a younger male singer "I want to hear you roll that 'r' *five times* before you finish the word!"

Lakmé - 2006

with Gaston Rivero, James Morris, Ellie Dehn, Wanda Brister, Daniel Mobbs, Yegishe Manucharyan, John Daly Goodwin (Choral Director), Stephanie Weiss. Seated: Heather Johnson, Eglise Gutiérrez, and Ira Siff (stage director). photo by Alix Barthelmes

Maestro Queler was one of the first conductors to truly believe in my talent and to this day, I'm eternally grateful for the faith she has in me as an artist. She has commanded an incredible legion of distinguished artists and must be commended for her assiduous dedication to maintaining the integrity and ethos of great music making in the traditional and correct way that opera ought to be performed, always. —Michael Fabiano

Michael Fabiano sang with me in 2006 in a supporting role in Donizetti's *Dom Sébastien*. After that, we did a number of smaller concerts together. Finally, in 2013, I was able to cast him in Verdi's *I Lombardi*. This was a great success

for him with critics and audience. Since then we have talked about another performance together but he has not been able to clear a date for OONY. His career has skyrocketed. I'm so proud to have been a part of that.

Dom Sébastien - 2006

with Mark Risinger, Michael Fabiano, Stephen Gaertner, Stephen Powell, Dmitry Korchak, Daniel Lewis William, Philip Cokorinos, and Vesselina Kasarova. photo by Alix Barthelmes

Eve has been a great champion of my career. She has always been a warm, open, and supportive figure during rehearsals and performances. Impassioned about the projects she chooses, there is always an electricity in her music making and preparations. Eve Queler is a truly lovely woman with a passion for the art form and is a pioneer for female conductors in the world of opera. —Angela Meade

photo by Karen W. Solorow

The first time I heard Angela Meade was at a competition where she sang the first section of "Casta Diva" from *Norma*. The color of her voice was exquisite as was her phrasing. She won first prize and proceeded to do the same in each succeeding competition she entered. In a few years, she was engaged to cover the leading role in Verdi's *Ernani* at the Met. As luck would have it, the soprano engaged to sing the role became ill, and Angela went on. I was in the audience at this extraordinary debut. According to Angela, that was the first complete role she had ever sung on stage.

I Lombardi - 2013

with Michael Fabiano and Angela Meade at Avery Fisher Hall.
photo courtesy of Stephanie Berger

I was finally able to invite Angela to sing in *I Lombardi* at Avery Fisher Hall in 2013 opposite Michael Fabiano. After that we decided to return to bel canto with a reprise of Donizetti's *Parisina d'Este* which I had introduced at the request of Montserrat Caballé in 1974. Angela showed herself to be the quintessential singer for this repertoire, using exquisite phrasing and ethereal high pianissimos.

In addition to featuring Angela in *Parisina,* I was happy to invite four young singers at the beginning of their careers: baritone Yunpeng Wang, bass Sava Vemic (on loan from the Metropolitan Opera Lindemann Young Artist Program), tenor Aaron Blake, and soprano Mia Pafumi. Yunpeng sang the role of Duke Azzo, an angry, hostile character with a beautiful introductory aria. He made a very strong impression with his characterization and powerful voice, with an easy top. Sava had already debuted with OONY in *Roberto Devereux,* and had been noticed by the audience and critics alike. Singing one of Donizetti's most difficult roles written for tenor voice, Aaron Blake showed that he has a sweet, subtle voice that he can color most expressively. There is only one supporting role in *Parisina d'Este,* the role of Imelda, which was sung by soprano Mia Pafumi, who received excellent reviews for her two ariettas.

Parisina d'Este - 2016

with Italo Marchini (chorus master), Aaron Blake, Angela Meade, Yunpeng Wang, Sava Vemic, and Mia Pafumi. photo by Fay Fox

Stephen Costello sang the small but significant role of the fisherman in Rossini's *William Tell*. The reason it is significant is because the fisherman opens the opera with a very pretty song which has a number of high C's. After that Stephen began singing at the Met. I heard him sing the role of Percy in *Anna Bolena*. I was finally able to get Stephen again for *Roberto Devereux* with Mariella Devia.

William Tell - 2005

with Patrick Carfizzi, Paul Mow, Philip Cokorinos, Christopher Burdette, Marcello Giordani, Marco Chingari, Stephen Costello, Malcolm Smith, Heather Johnson, Angela Maria Blasi, and Ellie Dehn. photo by Alix Barthelmes

Bryan Hymel understudied the title role in *Dom Sébastien,* a very high, specialized bel canto role. Bryan has appeared with me in a number of concerts including my annual opera series in the Berkshires. He had his official debut at Carnegie Hall with me and OONY at our 100th anniversary where he sang "La Donna e Mobile."

with Bryan Hymel.
photo by Philip Hageman

La Cenerentola - 1997

with Olga Makarina, Philip Cokorinos, Carla Wood, Bruce Fowler, Vivica
Genaux, Gino Quilico, and Eric Owens. photo by Alix Barthelmes

*I will always be grateful to Eve and the Opera Orchestra of New
York for giving me such wonderful opportunities to perform with
world-class singers in America's premier concert hall. Everyone
who has ever worked with Eve and OONY knows just how special
an experience it always is. I feel privileged to be a part of her OONY
family.* —Eric Owens

I Puritani - 1995

with Eric Owens, Dean Peterson, Carla Wood, Ron Naldi, Mariella
Devia, Gregory Kunde, and Carlo Guelfi. photo by Alix Barthelmes

22 - Agnes Varis - 2010

photo by Manuela Hoelterhoff

2010 was a year of highs and lows. OONY was forced to cancel performances due to a lack of funds. Then the Board of Directors selected a dynamic Italian maestro, Alberto Veronesi, to replace me as music director. Most significantly, my beloved Stanley was disappearing into dementia. He had been my rock, and had by now been moved to an assisted living facility. While I was contemplating all of this, I received the news that I was selected to receive the highest lifetime honor in opera from the National Endowment for the Arts.

I went off to Italy to conduct *Madama Butterfly* at the Puccini Festival in Torre del Lago. One day while I was at the theater, my cell phone rang, and it was Debbie Surdi, OONY's general manager. She asked if I was sitting down. I became worried that something had happened to Stanley. "No," she said, "it's good news." The good news was that Agnes Varis had contacted our office to tell us that she would contribute $250,000 so that I could conduct *L'Africaine* at Avery Fisher Hall in Lincoln Center.

It was a wonderful surprise to say the least. I had never met Ms. Varis, although I certainly knew her name as the great philanthropist who made it possible for 200 young people to attend the Met every night for $20 while she paid the difference for the most expensive seats. Ms. Varis had read in the *New York Times* that OONY was coming back after a break in performances. She was excited and wanted to do something to honor her late husband Karl Leichtman, who had died the year before and was a great fan of mine. Ms. Varis wrote me that her husband thought I walked on water.

I was thrilled to dedicate the performance to Karl. I was moved to discover how much Agnes and I had in common. As I got to know her, I found out that our husbands both suffered from Alzheimer's disease. We also found out that we shared the same birthday, just one year apart. She often signed her emails to me, "Sisters in Capricorn."

I was floored by Agnes's generous gift, but the gift of her friendship was also profoundly meaningful to me. We shared the story of our lives over long lunches, and she urged me to focus on my role as a *woman* conductor. I was brokenhearted to lose this very dear new friend only a year after we met, but her strength and wisdom remain an inspiration.

L'Africaine - 2011

with Ellie Dehn, Italo Marchini, Marcello Giordani, Chiara Taigi, Daniel Mobbs, Fikile Mvinjelwa, Lazaro Calderon, Gabriela Garcia, Djore Nance, Harold Wilson, and Giovanni Guagliardo. photo by Joyce Ravid

23 - NEA Honor

The memory of Eve Queler conducting concert operas in my growing up years is indelible. She introduced me to seldom-staged operatic gems, and showed me what women can do, at least as well as men, given the chance. —Justice Ruth Bader Ginsburg

One of the greatest thrills of my life was being honored by the National Endowment for the Arts in the fall of 2010 at The Kennedy Center. Only two other conductors before me had received this award: James Levine and Julius Rudel. The event was a pageant of presentations, speeches, performances, and receptions, beginning with a luncheon hosted by four Supreme Court justices at The Supreme Court Building. In attendance were Justices Ruth Bader Ginsburg, Antonin Scalia, Anthony Kennedy, and Elena Kagan. My fellow honorees, Martina Arroyo, Philip Glass, David DiChiera, and I gathered privately with our hosts prior to the lunch. I was especially moved to meet Justices Ginsburg and Scalia, whose famous friendship and love for opera provided another testament to the power of music to cross lines and bring people together.

We then entered the dining room with appropriate pomp and circumstance, where we were greeted by our friends and family. I was delighted that my daughter Liz, my grandson Joey, and my dear friend Gerald Rupp were able to join me at our table, hosted by the charming and distinguished Justice Kennedy. Joey was, at the time, a sixth grader at Hunter Elementary School, Justice Kagan's alma mater, where the halls were festooned with tributes celebrating her recent appointment to the bench. Joey was particularly excited to have a moment to present her with a tote bag filled with Hunter goodies (teddy bear, hoodie, mug, etc.) and I was so proud to offer him this unique experience.

with Justice Kagan and Joey Farber

After the sumptuous lunch, Justice Ginsburg invited me to her private office, where the first thing I saw was a large poster of Renée Fleming! There were also posters of *La Boheme, Tosca,* and other operas. What an amazing lady and how fortunate I was to have the opportunity to meet her and share some time.

Later that evening, Justice Ginsburg took the stage at The Kennedy Center, opening the award ceremony with three strikes of her gavel. A wonderful program ensued with each of the four honorees speaking and being presented with a beautiful memoir and a musical homage with voice and orchestra. My tribute was given by Ira Siff, host of the weekly Saturday broadcasts from the Met, and the fabulous Dolora Zajick sang an aria from one of my favorite operas, *La Favorita.*

It was extraordinary to be honored in such a way and in such esteemed company.

24 - Coda

Over the years, I've been called a groundbreaker, a trailblazer, a pioneer. But to this day, it's hard for me to embrace those titles. I had always been driven by my love for music, and that passion forged my path. Whether I laughed at, cried because of, or simply ignored the naysayers, I didn't spend time contemplating the obstacles. I followed the music and remained confident that my talent would open doors. Ultimately, conducting engagements took me on adventures to six continents, sharing stages with some of the finest singers in the world. It's been an incredible journey.

To a large degree, the lack of opportunities for women pianists, not to mention conductors, back in the 1950s and 1960s, forced me to carve out a place for myself. Ironically, that lack of opportunity led to a unique career path I never would have discovered had I been a man, and which I wouldn't have traded for the world. Never could I have dreamed when I founded Opera Orchestra that we would survive more than fifty years on one of the greatest stages in the world. I was simply looking for the next step forward. We realized quickly, however, that we had struck gold by creating something extraordinary that singers, musicians, and audiences in New York were craving. In addition to providing me a podium, OONY opened up a world of musical exploration.

I spent thrilling decades mining the incredibly rich annals of the opera repertoire, often unearthing rare gems. Bringing these works to life was exhilarating and a shared experience on every level. From the performers, to the audience, to the board, to the young singers I nurtured along the way, we took these musical voyages together.

I have always marveled at the power of music—to bridge language and cultural barriers, to express emotions words simply can't express, to enrapture and enthrall, to help us endure the hardships that we all face in our lives. I consider myself supremely fortunate to have experienced a lifetime of magical moments listening to and making music. To everyone who traveled with me— thank you, thank you, thank you!

And finally, to my young female colleagues, I say: be the best musician you can be . . . and follow the music!

Acknowledgements

I was fortunate to have the early guidance of John Gutman, Joseph Rosenstock, and Julius Rudel.

I'm so grateful for the devotion, generosity of time, and financial support of our OONY Board through the years. Our ten wonderful presidents were Marie Ashdown, Leon Fassler, Charles Cossey, Thomas Pulling, Albert Hudes, Richard Karl Goeltz, William Miller, William Scott, Alfred Hubay, and Norman Raben.

Other active board members were Gerald Rupp, Joan Sarnoff, Norma Litton, Joan Ades, Dr. Robert Campbell, Loeber Landau, Gordon Greenfield, Gideon Gartner, G. Morris Gurley, Clarice Kampel, Earle Kazis, Laura Scheuer, Leigh Raben, Terence McNally, Eva Popper, Frederic Bradley, Malcolm Graff, June LeBell, and Dorothy Szuch. Many became my friends. Most of the OONY board members remained for many, many years.

with Dr. Robert Campbell
and Anna Moffo

with Span and Marie Ashdown

Special thanks to my dear friend Marie Ashdown. She has consistently shown enormous support to me throughout my career, initially as OONY's first president, and more recently as executive director of the Musician's Emergency Fund.

Many thanks to the gracious Joan Ades, whose generosity allowed OONY to present *Parisina D'Este* in the Rose Theatre.

Deepest appreciation to Gerald Rupp for giving us the Vidda concert series and for his loving friendship.

Great thanks to my dear manager, Bob Lombardo who came into my life while OONY was still at Alice Tully Hall. His knowledge of the opera repertoire has been incredibly helpful to me. His musical taste, his love for the voice, and his friendship to both Stanley and me have been a huge blessing in my life.

I have also been very fortunate to have the assistance of my close friend Elizabeth Cole almost from the beginning of my concerts. She has been vocal coach, language coach, opera historian, and much more, assisting me backstage at every concert.

I would like to thank members of the OONY staff who have become family to me: assistant conductors Douglas Martin and Benton Hess, choral director Italo Marchini, executive director Deborah Surdi, business manager Tom Weatherly, personal assistant Keith Viagas, and office assistant Gina Dodds.

with Henry Schuman (first oboe), Eugene Moye (principal cello), Veronica Salas (principal viola) and Erica Kiesewetter (concertmaster). photo by Alix Barthelmes

I cannot find enough words to praise all of the brilliant musicians who have played for me over the years. Special thanks to my principals: Erica Kiesewetter, Veronica Salas, Eugene Moye, Steve Hartman, Henry Schuman, Ben Herman, Melanie Feld, and Dan Haskins.

For their help with this book, Bernette Jaffe and my good friends John Roberts and Lewis Ehlers.

I also want to express my appreciation to the Gerda Lissner Foundation, its president Stephen DeMaio, and Board of Directors Michael Fornabaio, Karl Michaelis, and Barbara Testa.

Our concerts could not have taken place without these wonderful choruses: The Schola Cantorum, The Coast Guard Academy Chorus, The West Point Cadet Glee Club, Princeton Pro Musica, Oratorio Society of New York, Ars Musica Chorale of New Jersey, Dessoff Choirs, The Mendelssohn Club of Philadelphia, Huntington Choral Society, Valley Forge Military Academy Chorus, New York Gay Men's Chorus, The Dallas Symphony Chorus, The Brooklyn Chorus, and The New York Choral Society. I am equally grateful to their directors: Hugh Ross, Robert de Cormier, John Daly Goodwin, Lyndon Woodside, William Noll, Tamara Brooks, Amy Kaiser, Frances Slade, Harry Saltzman, David Davidson, Benton Hess, Douglas Martin, and Italo Marchini.

I also want to thank my daughter Liz and my son-in-law Seth Farber for reviewing this book and helping me rewrite and clarify some of the events. Liz accompanied me on several trips and attended almost all of the performances in New York.

with Seth, Joey, and Liz. photo by Judy Pantino

with Sophie

Loving thanks to my family: my children Andy and Liz, her husband Seth, and my grandchildren Sam, Sophie, and Joey.

To my parents Harriet and Benjamin J. Rabin, who gave me the opportunity to pursue my dream.

I have not yet thanked the people who made my years of conducting such a success: the opera fans! There is nothing to compare with the enthusiasm and appreciation of our OONY audience.

To my wonderful husband Stanley, for his unending love and devotion. How lucky I was to have his support and encouragement for so many years. I could never imagine any of this happening without him by my side.

photo by Liz Queler

~ after party moments ~

with Joan Sarnoff

with Karl Michaelis, Gloria Gari,
and Barbara Testa

with Rev. John Kamas SSS
and Sir Cesare Santeramo

with Gerald Rupp
and John Roberts

with Stephen DeMaio

with Murray Rosenthal

with Doug Martin

with Glenn Morton, Debbie Surdi and
Michael Fornabaio. photo by Judy Pantano

 # Honors and Awards

National Endowment for the Arts 2010 Opera Honoree

Chevalier de l'Ordre des Arts et des Lettres

Gerda Lissner Foundation
Opera Index Award
Career Bridges Foundation
Touchstone Award - Women In Music, Inc.
Sanford Fellowship - Yale University
Special Citation - Metropolitan Chapter of the Victorian Society
     in America for 35 Years of Concert Performances of
     Neglected 19th Century Operas
Verdi America Award from the American Institute of Verdi
     Studies at New York University
Metropolitan Opera Club
Honorary Doctorate - Russell Sage College
Honorary Doctorate - Colby College
The National Arts Club
The National Opera Association
Woman of Achievement Award - Washington Square
     Business and Professional Women's Club
Musician of the Month - Musical America Magazine
Eagle Award - The Licia Albanese-Puccini Foundation
Butterfly Award - The Licia Albanese-Puccini Foundation
The Richard Tucker Music Foundation Award
The Dewar's Profile

OONY Performance History
Conducted by Eve Queler

Mar. 13, 1972	Rossini - *William Tell*	Barlow, Toscano, Morris, Quilico, Lo Monaco
Apr. 20, 1972	Meyerbeer - *L'Africana*	Stella, Tucker, Elgar, Manuguerra
Dec. 7, 1972	Verdi - *I Lombardi*	Scotto, Carreras, Marini, Plishka
Mar. 22, 1973	Zandonai - *Francesca Da Rimini*	Domingo, Kabaivanska, Manuguerra, Saetta
Jan. 20, 1974	Bizet - *Les Pêcheurs De Perles*	Gedda, Bruson, Eda-Pierre
Mar. 6, 1974	Donizetti - *Parisina D'Este*	Caballé, Chudy, Pruett, Morris, Quilico
Feb. 12, 1975	Verdi - *I Masnadieri*	Trombin, Lewis, Manuguerra, Plishka
Feb. 26, 1975	Donizetti - *La Favorita*	Verrett, Kraus, Elvira, Hendricks, Morris
Dec. 11, 1975	Berlioz - *Lelio,* + Arias	Aler, Burchinal, Scotto
Mar. 8, 1976	Massenet - *Le Cid*	Domingo, Bumbry, Plishka, Voketaitis
Mar. 14, 1976	Donizetti - *Gemma Di Vergy*	Caballé, Lima, Quilico, Plishka, Chudy
Jan. 9, 1977	Smetana - *Dalibor*	Kubiak, Gedda, Monk, Plishka, Sormova
Apr. 13, 1977	Puccini - *Edgar*	Scotto, Bergonzi, Killebrew, Sardinero
Feb. 23, 1978	Weber - *Oberon*	Gedda, Jones, Hamari, West
Mar. 14, 1978	Rossini - *Tancredi*	Ricciarelli, Horne, Palacio, Zaccaria
Feb. 25, 1979	Janáček - *Kátya Kabanová*	Beňačková, Chudy, Martinovich, Kniplova, Lewis
Apr. 8, 1979	Verdi - *Aroldo*	Caballé, Cecchele, Pons,
May 13, 1979	Bellini - *I Capuleti Ed I Montecchi*	Troyanus, Tenzi, Putnam, Robbins
Feb. 6, 1980	Massenet - *Hérodiade*	Plishka, Malamood, Pons, Verdejo, Greevy

Mar. 10, 1980	Donizetti - *Lucrezia Borgia*	Ricciarelli, Gonzalez, Manuguerra
Apr. 10, 1980	Wagner - *Rienzi*	Payer, Hamari, Sooter
Mar. 1, 1981	Moussorgsky - *Khovanshchina*	Toczyska, Plishka, Kazaras, Monk, Gulyas, Alexieva
Apr. 13, 1981	Delibes - *Lakmé*	Devia, Gedda, Spacagna, Plishka,
Jun. 13, 1981	Mercadante - *Il Giuramento*	Gulyas, Zampieri, Baltsa, Martin
Oct. 20, 1981	Verdi - *I Due Foscari*	Bergonzi, Bruson, Castro-Alberti, Ryerson
Feb. 28, 1982	Wagner - *Rienzi*	Payer, Hamari, Johns, Massey, Warner
Mar. 3, 1982	Wagner - *Rienzi*	Evans, Hamari, Johns.
		The Kennedy Center
Apr. 12, 1982	Boito - *Nerone*	Andrade, Takács, Elvira, Morris, LaCiura, Cigoj
Oct. 28, 1982	Donizetti - *Il Duca D'Alba*	Krilovici, Gonzalez, Manuguerra
Jan. 21, 1983	Strauss - *Guntram*	Goldberg, Yule, Tokody, Roloff, Kazaras
May 8, 1983	Berlioz - *Benvenuto Cellini*	Gedda, Devia, Vento, Lafont, Boozer
Nov. 6, 1983	Strauss - *Die Liebe Der Danae*	Plowright, Blackwell, Ulfung, Kazaras, Roloff
Mar. 23, 1984	Donizetti - *Dom Sébastien*	Leech, Takács, Kopchak, Miller
May 13, 1984	Verdi - *Nabucco*	Dimitrova, Schuman, Monk, Pinto, Plishka
Oct. 29, 1984	Glinka - *A Life for the Tsar*	Kopchak, Markova, Merritt, Talvela
Nov. 20, 1984	Rossini - *William Tell*	Evstatieva, Bonisolli, Cappuccilli, Hunter
Apr. 15, 1985	Lalo - *Le Roi D'Ys*	Hendricks, Ciurca, Titus, Raffalli
Jan. 19, 1986	Verdi - *I Lombardi*	Millo, Bergonzi, Plishka
Mar. 13, 1986	Smetana - *Libuše*	Beňačková, Roark-Strummer, Plishka
May 6, 1986	Ponchielli - *La Gioconda*	Dimitrova, Cappuccilli, Plishka, Milcheva, Lamberti
Jan. 12, 1987	Verdi - *La Battaglia Di Legnano*	Millo, Garcia, Malagnini, Manuguerra, Hopkins, Watson
Feb. 22, 1987	Wagner - *Ring Cycle Excerpts*	Marton, Bean, Roloff, Barr
May 6, 1987	Dvořák - *Rusalka*	Beňačková, Kelm, Kopchak,

Feb. 21, 1988	Meyerbeer - *Robert Le Diable*	Mims, Merritt, Ginsberg, Laciura, Ramey
Mar. 13, 1988	Giordano - *Andrea Chénier*	Millo, Bean, Polozov, Salvadori Shaulis
Mar. 30, 1988	Janáček - *Jenůfa*	Beňačková, Rysanek, Kazaras, Ochman,
Oct. 27, 1988	Bellini - *Beatrice Di Tenda*	Anderson, Zseller, Tumagian, Kiurkciev
Jan. 29, 1989	Giordano - *Fedora*	Marton, Blackwell, Todisco, Serrano
Mar. 2, 1989	Bellini - *Il Pirata*	Fleming, Kunde, Robertson, Moore

John Harms Center, Englewood, New Jersey

Mar. 6, 1989	Bellini - *Il Pirata*	Millo, Liang, Morino, Croft
Jan. 16, 1990	Verdi - *I Vespri Siciliani*	Dunn, Brubaker, Glassman, Bruson, Plishka
Feb. 28, 1990	Tchaikovsky - *Maid Of Orleans*	Kopchak, Zajick, Kulko
Apr. 17, 1990	Catalani - *La Wally*	Millo, Manuguerra, Jóhannsson, Zambalis
Jan. 9, 1991	Donizetti - *Roberto Devereux*	Rowland, Zambalis, de la Mora, Chernov
Feb. 10, 1991	Bellini - *La Sonnambula*	Anderson, Keith, Plishka, Giménez
Mar. 28, 1991	Weber - *Der Freischütz*	Behrens, Giering, Sotin, Heppner
Jan. 30, 1992	Boieldieu - *La Dame Blanche*	Fleming, Uecker, Swenson, Charbonneau
Mar. 15, 1992	Wagner - *Rienzi*	Pick-Hieronimi, Goldberg, Graham, Kokorinos, Röschmann
Apr. 5, 1992	Verdi - *I Due Foscari*	Rowland, Villa, Chernov, Barr, Short,
Feb. 7, 1993	Bellini - *La Straniera*	Fleming, Liang, Kunde, Laperriere
Apr. 7, 1993	Donizetti - *Anna Bolena*	Vaness, Scalchi, de la Mora, Plishka, Cokorinos
May 2, 1993	Tchaikovsky - *Mazeppa*	Anderson, Grigorian, Leiferkus, Plishka
Dec. 19, 1993	Donizetti - *Linda Di Chamounix*	Esposito, Sabbatini, Frontali, Poretsky, Plishka
Feb. 15, 1994	Bellini - *I Capuleti Ed I Montecchi*	Devia, Giménez, Spagnoli, Larmore
Mar. 13, 1994	Donizetti - *Caterina Cornaro*	Rowland, d'Auria, Bruson, Colombara

Feb. 14, 1995	Massenet - *Hérodiade*	Fleming, Bumbry, Del Campo, Owens
Mar. 5, 1995	Rimsky-Korsakov - *The Tsar's Bride*	Borodina, Focile, Uhlenhopp, Leiferkus, Plishka
May 8, 1995	Bellini - *I Puritani*	Devia, Kunde, Wood, Owens, Guelfi
Dec. 11, 1995	Bellini - *Norma*	Eaglen, Ganassi, di Renzi, Anisimov
Apr. 17, 1996	Rossini - *Armida*	Fleming, Kunde, Fowler, Cokorinos
May 8, 1996	Verdi - *Giovanna D'Arco*	Anderson, Grigorian, Moore, Guelfi, Owens
Jan. 12, 1997	Rossini - *La Cenerentola*	Makarina, Genaux, Fowler, Owens, Quilico, Wood
Feb. 9, 1997	Wagner - *Tristan Und Isolde*	Connell, Siukola, Ryerson, Breault, Brainerd, Lang
Apr. 6, 1997	Verdi - *Ernani*	Anderson, Margison, Guelfi, Plishka
Nov. 23, 1997	Rossini - *Tancredi*	Kasarova, O'Flynn, Breault, Wood
Feb. 8, 1998	Verdi - *Jerusalem*	Valayre, Simpson, Ikaia-Purdy, Ramey, Cokorinos
May 4, 1998	Donizetti - *Poliuto*	Rowland, Armiliato, Meoni, Alberghini
Mar. 7, 1999	Verdi - *I Masnadieri*	Nagore, Wolf, Hvorostovsky, Plishka, Konstantinov
Apr. 13, 1999	Halévy - *La Juive*	Papian, Casanova, Corvino, Ruminski, Plishka, Makarina
May 12, 1999	Bellini - *La Sonnambula*	Swenson, Wood, Tapia, Kunde, Relyea
Oct. 25, 1999	Bellini - *I Capuleti Ed I Montecchi*	Massis, Kasarova, Kunde, Cokorinos, Carfizzi
Nov. 11, 1999	Donizetti - *Adelia*	Devia, Plishka, Pyatnychko, Mok
Feb. 14, 2000	Donizetti - *Lucrezia Borgia*	Fleming, Blythe, Giordani, Corvino
May 3, 2000	Verdi - *Otello*	Bergonzi, Barasorda, Esperian, Kitic, Plishka
Mar. 7, 2001	Donizetti - *La Favorita*	Hvorostovsky, Larmore, Kunde, Kowaljow
Apr. 23, 2001	Meyerbeer - *Les Huguenots* Stoyanova,	Giordani, Makarina, Zifchak, Simpson
May 13, 2001	Donizetti - *Maria Stuarda*	Swenson, Flanigan, Matos, Kunde
Nov. 13, 2001	Verdi - *La Battaglia Di Legnano*	Stoyanova, Casanova, Guelfi, Kowaljow

Mar. 3, 2002	Cilea - *Adriana Lecouvreur*	Millo, Zajick, Giordani, Golesorkhi
Apr. 21, 2002	Donizetti - *Marino Faliero*	Kunde, Lafontaine, Blancas, Relyea
Oct. 20, 2002	Bizet - *The Pearl Fishers*	Takova, Shtoda, Chaignaud, Faria
Apr. 25, 2003	Verdi - *Attila*	Flanigan, Casanova, Ramey, Grant
May 19, 2003	Rossini - *La Donna Del Lago*	Swenson, Blythe, Fowler, Trejo
Dec. 14, 2003	Donizetti - *Anna Bolena*	Larmore, Stoyanova, Manucharyan, Morris, Aldrich
Mar. 21, 2004	Verdi - *Il Corsaro*	Casanova, Dragoni, Potenza, Liao
Apr. 20, 2004	Ponchielli - *La Gioconda*	Millo, Giordani, Kitic, Golesorkhi
Nov. 22, 2004	Puccini - *La Fanciulla Del West*	Millo, Tanner, Chingari
Apr. 7, 2005	Thomas - *Mignon*	Gutiérrez, Blythe, Aldrich, Giordano, Relyea
Jun. 6, 2005	Von Weber - *Der Freischütz*	Margiono, Moon, Studebaker, Cokorinos, Kovaljow
Nov. 13, 2005	Rossini - *William Tell*	Blasi, Giordani, Chingari, Costello, Dehn
Feb. 28, 2006	Delibes - *Lakmé*	Gutiérrez, Morris, Johnson, Dehn, Manucharyan
May 4, 2006	Montemezzi - *L'Amore Di Tre Rei*	Bravo, de la Mora, Ramey, Baransky
Nov. 7, 2006	Donizetti - *Dom Sébastien*	Fabiano, Powell, Korchak, Kasarova, Cokorinos, Gaertner
Jan. 19, 2007	Rossini - *Otello*	Donose, Ford, Tarver, McPherson, Zifchak
Feb. 21, 2007	Cilea - *L'Arlesiana*	Moore, Filianoti, Cornetti
Dec. 13, 2007	Verdi - *I Due Foscari*	Di Giacomo, Gavanelli, Machado
Feb. 27, 2008	Bellini - *La Sonnambula*	Gutiérrez, Furlanetto, Korchak, Caballéro
Mar. 6, 2008	100th Performance Gala	Scott, Fleming, Millo, Giordani, Hymel, Mobbs, Gutiérrez, Gaertner
Apr. 13, 2008	Puccini - *Edgar*	Giordani, Moore, Larmore, Gaertner, Guagliardo
Oct. 15, 2008	Rimsky-Korsakov - *The Tsar's Bride*	Borodina, Makarina, Markov, Manucharyan, Stamboglis
Mar. 2, 2011	Meyerbeer - *L'Africaine*	Giordani, Taigi, Dehn, Mvinjelwa, Stayton
Jan. 29, 2012	Wagner - *Rienzi*	Storey, Chauvet, Matos, Cedel, DeVine

Apr. 8, 2013	Verdi - *I Lombardi*	Meade, Fabiano, Short, Baetge, Cedel
Jun. 5, 2014	Donizetti - *Roberto Devereux*	Devia, Costello, Chauvet, Vemic, Pershall
May 4, 2016	Donizetti - *Parisina D'Este*	Meade, Blake, Vemic, Wang, Pafumi
May 6, 2018	Gerda Lissner Foundation Awards Concert	

Working with Eve was one of my great New York experiences. To see not only her love for the music but also her great love for singers inspired us to give back as much care and love as we were given. She is a phenomenon in our world, and I will always treasure that concert in my heart.

—Carol Vaness

I Capuleti ed I Montecchi - 1994

with Julien Robbins, Pietro Spagnoli, Mariella Devia, Raul Giménez, and Jennifer Larmore. photo by Alix Barthelmes

Maria Stuarda - 2001

with C.Y. Liao, Lauren Flanagan, Gregory Kunde, Eleni Matos, Ruth
Ann Swenson, and Patrick Carfizzi. photo by Alix Barthelmes

Mignon - 2005

with Charles Unice, Kate Aldrich, Rubin Casas, John Relyea,
Stephanie Blythe, John Daly Goodwin, Massimo Giordano, Eglise
Gutiérrez, and William Ferguson. photo by Alix Barthelmes

with Matthew White. photo by Jeyran Ghara

Roberto Devereux - 2014

with Andre Courville, Mariella Devia, Stephen Costello, David Pershall, Geraldine Chauvet, John Kapusta, and Sava Vemic.

with Steve Hartman, Ben Herman, and Eugene Moye

Rienzi - 2012

with Emily Duncan Brown, Ian Storey, the children's chorus from The Special Music School and New York Choral Society. photo by Chris Lee

 Guest Conducting

Staged Opera

Puccini Festival, Torre del Lago, Italy, *Madama Butterfly*
Hamburg Opera, *Don Pasquale*
Liceu Theater Barcelona, *I Vespri Siciliani, Parisina D'Este*
Maryinsky Theatre, Russia, *Mazeppa*
Smetana Divadlo, Prague, *Carmen, Rigoletto*
Teatro Colon, Argentina, *Elisabetta Regina d'Inghilterra*
New York City Opera, *Le Nozze di Figaro*
Opera de Quebec, *Les Contes d'Hoffmann*
Las Palmas, Spain, *L'Elisir d'Amore, Fidelio*
Opera Bonn, *Jenůfa, La Traviata, Fidelio*
Australian Opera, Sydney, *Die Entfuhrung aus dem Serail*
Hamilton, Ontario, Canada, *Il Barbiere di Siviglia*
Macau Festival, China, *Otello*
Kassel Opera, *Der Fliegende Hollander*
Oberlin Opera Theatre, *Le Nozze di Figaro*
Opera of Pretoria, South Africa, *Les Contes d'Hoffmann*
San Diego Opera, *Anna Bolena*
Utah Opera, *La Boheme*
Lake George Opera, *La Boheme, Tosca*
Opera de Nice, *Parisina D'Este*
Brno Opera, *Jenůfa*
Jackson, MS, *Norma*
Chattanooga Opera, TN, *La Traviata*
Shreveport, LA, *The Tales of Hoffman*
Livorno Summer Festival, Italy, *Un Giorno di Regno*

Concert Opera

Orchestra de lo Stato de Mexico, *Otello, La Battaglia di Legnano, Les Huguenots, Les Pêcheurs de Perles*
New Philharmonia Orchestra, London, *I Puritani*
Aarhus, Denmark, *I Puritani*
Frankfurt Opera, *Tancredi*

Symphonic Programs

Rome Opera
Philadelphia Orchestra
Cleveland Orchestra
San Antonio Symphony
Temple University
SUNY Potsdam
Chautauqua Symphony
Orchestre Nationale L'Ile de France
Orchestra Lyrique de Paris
Orchestra Sinfonica Siciliana, Palermo
Puerto Rico Symphony
New Jersey Symphony
Edmonton Symphony
Toledo Symphony
Hartford Symphony
Kansas City Symphony
Colorado Springs Symphony
Jacksonville Symphony

Opera Galas

Teatro Massimo Bellini, Catania, Sicily - Bellini Festival
Palm Beach Opera Competitions Finals
Tivoli, **Italy**
Salle Pleyel, **Paris**
Honolulu Symphony
Montreal Symphony
Boston Symphony Hall - Aprile Millo
National Symphony, Washington DC - Aprile Millo
Wolf Trap Festival - Renata Scotto, Louis Quilico,
Brooklyn College - Renata Scotto, Sherrill Milnes
Tilles Center, **NY** - Aprile Millo
Mechanics Hall, **Worcester, MA** - Aprile Millo
Hong Kong Philharmonic
Carnegie Hall, NY - Olga Borodina and Dmitri Hvorostovsky
Carnegie Hall, **NY** - Ghena Dimitrova and Piero Cappuccilli
Carnegie Hall, **NY** - Renata Scotto
Tapia Theatre, San Juan PR - Justin Diaz

with Renata Scotto at Wolf Trap

Discography

Massenet, *Le Cid*
Bumbry, Domingo, Plishka, Queler
Live from Carnegie Hall
CBS Sony Music - M3K34211

Donizetti, *Gemma di Vergy*
Caballé, Lima, Quilico, Plishka, Queler
Live from Carnegie Hall
CBS - M3 34575

Puccini, *Edgar*
Scotto, Bergonzi, Queler
Live from Carnegie Hall
CBS M2K 34584

Verdi, *Aroldo*
Caballé, Cecchele, Pons, Queler,
Live from Carnegie Hall
CBS Masterworks 79328

Janáček, *Jenůfa*
Rysanek, Beňačková, Ochman, Kazaras
Queler, Conductor
Live from Carnegie Hall
BISCD-449/450 Stereo -

R.Strauss, *Guntram*
Ilona Tokody, Reiner Goldberg Eve
Queler, Conductor
Hungaroton - Sony Music

Boito, *Nerone*
Tokody, Takács, Nagy, Miller
Queler, Conductor
Hungaroton - Sony Music
HCD 12487-89-2

Wagner, *Tristan and Isolde*
Connell, Siukkola, Lang, Brainerd,
Ryerson, Breault
Queler, Conductor
Live from Carnegie Hall

CPSIA information can be obtained
at www.ICGtesting.com
Printed in the USA
BVHW071052100419
545158BV00003B/462/P

9 781984 566829